THE
BEGINNER'S
COOKBOOK

Basic, easy-to-follow recipes for first-time cooks

Linda Venturoni-Wilson

**HARBOUR
BOOKS**

Contents

Basic cooking terms

Al dente: an Italian term generally applied to the cooking of pasta. Translated it means "to the tooth", meaning pasta should be firm when bitten, not soft.

Baste: to spoon liquid (usually fat, oil, stock or cooking juices) over food during cooking to prevent drying out e.g. roast meat and kebabs.

Blanch: commonly used to mean pre-cook or parboil (partially cook) vegetables for a short time so they need little or no further cooking.

Boil: to cook in liquid at boiling point; boiling point of water is 212°F (100°C). The water should be bubbling rapidly, as distinct from simmering (see page 5).

Braise: to cook meat and vegetables by sautéing in fat and then cooking slowly in very little moisture.

Broil (grill): a method of cooking by exposing food to dry heat, either from gas or an electric stove broiler (grill). Uses red coals of a barbecue or outdoor fire, surface of a griddle pan heated on a stove or an open fire.

Court bouillon: a light stock, made from vegetables and herbs, used mainly for poaching fish or shellfish.

Deep-fry: to cook in a deep, heavy-based pan in sufficient fat or oil to cover food completely. Used for foods requiring a brief time to cook e.g. fish fillets, French fries and fritters.

Deglaze: to heat liquid (usually stock and/or wine) in a dish or pan stirring to scrape up sediment that remains after roasting or frying. This forms the base of a sauce.

Degorge: to extract juices from vegetables (e.g. eggplant/aubergine) by salting, then soaking or rinsing, to remove excess moisture or bitter juices. If you prefer not to use salt, soak eggplant (aubergine) for 45 minutes in a large bowl of acidulated water — cold water mixed with the juice of 1 lemon — to achieve similar results. Not all eggplant requires degorging. Usually just larger, older specimens.

Dice: to cut meat, cheese or vegetables into small ($1/8$–$1/4$ in/3–5 mm) or large (1–$1\frac{1}{3}$ in/2–3 cm) cubes using a sharp knife.

Fold: to combine a light, whisked or creamed mixture with a heavier mixture so that lightness is retained. Use a metal spoon or spatula to cut down through the mixture, across the bottom of the bowl, then up and over, close to the surface — turn the bowl frequently.

Grease (pans, etc.): use melted butter or oil applied with a brush or buttered paper, or non-stick oil sprays, if preferred.

Herbs: to use dried herbs, measure the amount needed onto your hand then crush to release the flavor before adding to a dish. To substitute fresh herbs for dried, triple the amount of the fresh.

Julienne: to cut food (e.g. vegetables, citrus rind, ham) into thin matchsticks or very fine shreds.

Marinade: seasoned mixture (generally of oil and wine) or a sauce with herbs and other flavorings in which meat or fish is left to stand (marinate) for some hours or overnight before cooking. This gives flavor and sometimes tenderizes the food.

Reduce: to boil a mixture, uncovered, until the quantity is reduced and the flavor concentrated.

Refresh: cooked foods, mainly vegetables, are passed quickly under or immersed in cold water to stop the cooking process and preserve color.

Sauté: to fry quickly in a shallow pan over high temperature. The food must be completely dry before cooking and cooked in small batches to brown well. A combination of butter and oil is commonly used — butter adds flavor and color and the oil prevents the butter scorching.

Sear: to brown meat quickly on both sides to seal in juices; the heat is usually then lowered for the remaining cooking time.

Seasoned flour: all-purpose (plain) flour to which salt and pepper have been added. Usually used to protect foods from high cooking heats e.g frying.

Shallow-fry: to cook in a small quantity of fat or oil in a shallow pan. Used for foods which take a comparatively long time to cook, such as sausages, schnitzels, thick pieces of fish or whole fish.

Simmer: to bring food in liquid to the boil, then to reduce heat and keep the food cooking slowly, just below boiling point, at about 180°F (82°C) so that the liquid bubbles gently. Suitable for casseroles and dishes requiring long, slow cooking.

Skim: to remove scum or fat from the surface of a liquid, using a slotted spoon or mesh ladle.

Steam: to cook food in the steam from boiling water, using a perforated utensil, usually made from either bamboo or metal and positioned over a pot or pan.

Stir-fry: to cook over high heat, stirring or tossing the food constantly, with a wok spoon (wok chan) in a wok. A large, deep frying pan can also be used.

Sweat: to cook food gently in butter or oil in a tightly covered pan over very low heat. Generally used for vegetables, particularly onions. The slow cooking develops flavor.

Tray-freeze: place room-temperature item (do not wrap) on tray and freeze until solid. Wrap in plastic, return to freezer and freeze up to 2 months. Suitable for cakes.

To use a meat thermometer: insert in center of meat so that bulb reaches thickest part, ensuring it does not rest on bone or fat. Roast meat and, when gauge registers desired degree, push thermometer slightly further into meat. If temperature drops, continue cooking; if temperature is maintained, the meat is done.

ROASTING GUIDE FOR BEEF AND LAMB

	Cooking Time (per 1 lb/500 g)	Internal Temperature
Rare	20–25 minutes	140°F (60°C)
Medium	25–30 minutes	160°F (70°C)
Well-done	30–35 minutes	170°F (76°C)

Storage tips

THE FREEZER
• Use good-quality foods, well prepared and carefully wrapped.
• Set the freezer to 0°F (-18°C) or lower for long-term storage of pre-prepared meals; leftovers that would otherwise be wasted; inexpensive seasonal fruits and vegetables; meat, poultry and seafood bargains; homebaked breads and cakes; home-made stock.
• Wrap food in air-tight, moisture-proof plastic or foil containers, heavily waxed cartons, ice cream containers, plastic freezer wrap and food bags or heavy-duty foil. Remove as much air as possible to prevent moisture loss which causes "freezer burn". When storing liquid or semi-liquid foods, allow $\frac{1}{2}$–1 in (1–2.5 cm) space at top of container for expansion during freezing.
• Label and date foods. Keep a freezer inventory.
• To thaw — thaw foods slowly in the refrigerator over 24 hours or in a microwave following manufacturer's directions. Generally, thawed foods must not be refrozen.

WHAT TO FREEZE
• **Breads:** Wrap in foil or plastic. Freeze no longer than 2 months as flavor begins to deteriorate. Thaw at room temperature on a wire rack. If desired, refresh thawed bread by wrapping in foil and heating in 300°F (150°C) oven, 20–30 minutes.
• **Cakes:** Tray-freeze (see page 5); wrap in plastic or waxed (greaseproof) paper; pack in sturdy cartons. Do not frost unless using butter-based icings. Freeze up to 2 months. Thaw at room temperature on a wire rack. Frost before serving.
• **Cookies:** Tray-freeze; pack in plastic bags or containers. Freeze up to 3 months. Thaw at room temperature.

• **Dairy products:** Freeze only the freshest cream in original containers up to 3 months. (Thawed cream is only suitable for whipping.) Freeze butter, margarine and cooking fats in original wrappings overwrapped in foil or plastic for 3–6 months. Divide hard cheese into useable portions, wrap in thick plastic and freeze up to 6 months.
• **Fish and shellfish:** Scale and clean; rinse under cold water. Leave fish whole only if to be cooked whole, otherwise cut into fillets or steaks (cutlets) and tray-freeze (see page 5). Wrap separately before storing in sturdy bags or containers. Place shrimp (prawns) in sturdy container and fill with water, leaving $\frac{3}{4}$ in (2 cm) space at the top. Freeze white-fleshed fish 3–4 months; oily fish and shellfish no more than 3 months.
• **Fruit:** Do not freeze bruised, under-ripe or over-ripe fruit. Freeze whole small fruit (e.g berries) in dry sugar or syrup, or as puree, or tray-freeze without sugar. Pack in sturdy cartons, leaving space if syrup-packed. Large fruit must be stoned (pitted) or cored and peeled. Pack as above. Freeze up to 6 months. Thaw in refrigerator or at room temperature.
• **Meat and poultry:** Pre-packaged items can be frozen for 1–2 weeks in original wrappings. For longer storage, see below.
— *Individual pieces* (e.g steaks, poultry pieces.). Wrap separately in foil or waxed (greaseproof) paper, freeze flat, then wrap in meal-size portions in freezer bags. Freeze up to 6 months. Thaw steak before cooking, or if you like meat cooked rare to medium, you can cook without thawing — brush with oil or butter and broil (grill) on high heat 3 minutes first side then 2 minutes other side. Cook first side again — 1 minute more for rare, 2–3 minutes on medium heat for medium steak.

— *Ground (minced) meat, sausages, vacuum-packed bacon or ham.* Freeze no longer than 1 month. Thaw completely before cooking.

— *Whole poultry or meat joints.* Never stuff poultry before freezing. Freeze 4–6 months. To thaw, loosen wrappings to allow air circulation. Place poultry or joint on rack over drip tray and thaw in refrigerator.

— *Cooked meat dishes.* Use seasonings sparingly as flavors intensify in freezer. Do not overcook initially as meat fibers will shred on reheating. Line a suitably-sized dish with freezer-proof bag or double thickness of foil, allowing enough overhang to cover food completely. Cool cooked food quickly, transfer to prepared container, cover and freeze. When solid, remove bag or foil from container, expel air, seal well and return to freezer. Freeze 2–3 months.

• **Stock, soup and sauces:** chill cooked mixtures quickly over ice water; skim off any fat. Store in sturdy containers leaving space for expansion. Freeze concentrated stock in ice cube trays then transfer cubes to a plastic bag. Freeze for 2–3 months. Thaw in saucepan over low heat, or drop cubes into cooked mixtures as needed.

• **Vegetables:** blanch in boiling water before freezing. Pack in moisture-proof, air-tight bags or containers, removing all air. Freeze 6–8 months. Cook (steam, boil, microwave etc.) directly from frozen state.

THE REFRIGERATOR

Perishables to be used within a few days should be stored in the refrigerator at temperatures between 36–40°F (2–5°C).

• **Fruit:** some fruit benefits from brief storage at cool room temperature to finish the ripening process. Fully ripened fruit is best refrigerated in loosely covered containers or in ventilated food storage bags to prevent wilting or drying. Those with thick skins, such as melons, avocados and pineapple, do not need wrapping. Keep berries dry. Do not refrigerate bananas.

• **Vegetables:** fresh vegetables will stay fresh for up to 7 days if stored, wrapped in moisture-proof food storage bags, in the refrigerator crisper. Wash and thoroughly drain salad greens, wrap in paper towels and seal in plastic food bags. Discard leafy tops from beets, radishes or carrots before storing. Keep mushrooms in cloth or paper bags to prevent sweating. Do not refrigerate potatoes, onions, garlic, and winter squash (pumpkin). These vegetables are best stored unwashed in a cool, dry, dark well-ventilated place.

• **Dairy foods:** refrigerate cheese, milk and butter tightly covered to prevent odors penetrating.

• **Meat and poultry:** fresh items can be stored in original wrappings for 1–2 days. If longer refrigeration is necessary (up to 3–4 days), loosen wrappings at both ends. Rewrap fresh meat loosely in waxed (greaseproof) paper. Cool and refrigerate cooked meat promptly. Cover to prevent drying.

• **Other foods:** nuts keep better if refrigerated in air-tight containers. Canned foods, once opened, should be transferred to sealed containers and refrigerated. Store eggs in their original carton.

THE PANTRY

Staples, both packaged and canned, store best at room temperature — between 50 and 70°F (10–21°C) — in a cool, dry, airy place away from direct sunlight or heat.

• **Packaged items:** dried beans, peas and lentils, rice, pasta, breakfast cereals, flour, leavenings, dried fruit and the like are best stored in sealable plastic or glass containers to keep moisture and insects out.

• **Canned items:** never buy bulging or damaged cans as contents may be spoiled.

Equipment

HAND TOOLS

• knives — paring (long and short-bladed, one serrated), cleaver (chopper), carver
• graduated measuring spoons and cups, 2-cup jug, scales (optional), slotted spoon, tongs, wooden spoons, spaghetti spoon (optional), eggflip (pancake turner), whisk, meat fork, ladle, kitchen shears, flexible-bladed metal spatulas (long and short), rubber spatula (scraper), flat fish server, can opener, potato masher, vegetable peeler, apple corer

UTENSILS

• mixing — glass or metal bowls of graduated sizes
• baking — oven gloves or cloth, sifter or sieve, baking sheets, pie pan (flan ring) with removable base, fluted quiche dish, pie dishes (1 fruit plate, 1 oval dish for meat), springform or round cake pans, square pan, muffin pan, loaf pan, wire cooling rack
• roasting — roasting pan, roasting rack, baking dish with lid, meat thermometer
• stove-top cooking — saucepans with lids: small (with pouring spout), medium and large, double boiler insert (or heatproof bowl to fit pan), deep-fry basket insert (optional); frying pans (large and small, nonstick), crepe/omelette pan, oval fish poacher/kettle (optional), wok and wok chan, flameproof casserole dish with lid (preferably cast iron)

ACCESSORIES

• paper towels, foil, greaseproof (waxed) paper, baking (parchment) paper, plastic food wrap and bags
• 2–3 cutting boards
• citrus juicer
• screw-top jar for dressings, salad bowl and servers
• sieve (1 small, 1 large), colander
• metal steamer insert or bamboo or metal steamer
• grater (shredder)
• bamboo and metal skewers, toothpicks, kitchen string
• brushes for pastry and basting
• ramekins for use in microwave (for melting, etc.)
• egg rings, egg poacher (optional)

APPLIANCES

• hand-held electric mixer, small blender, standard food processor

(1) citrus juicer (2) muffin pan (3) serrated knife (4) carving knife (5) paring knife (6) pie pan (flan ring) (7) roasting pan (8) spaghetti spoon (9) basting brush (10) eggflip (pancake turner) (11) whisk (12) rubber spatula (scraper) (13) wooden spoon (14) sieve (15) baking sheet (16) grater (shredder) (17) saucepan (18) measuring cups (19) jug (20) colander (21) frying pan (22) measuring spoons (23) springform cake pan (24) pastry brush

Pantry checklist

A well-stocked pantry and small supply of a few fresh, refrigerated items provide the basis for impromptu, hazzle-free meals.

It's a good idea to plan a few menus in advance and purchase in bulk food you use frequently. Store older items at the front of shelves and replace those with expired use-by dates.

HERBS, SPICES AND SEASONINGS

• plant pots or a mini garden with a few essentials — chives, parsley, basil, cilantro (coriander)
• dried herbs — oregano, thyme, sage, rosemary, dill, bay leaves
• spices — salt, black pepper, ground cinnamon, nutmeg, mixed spice, chili flakes or cayenne pepper, paprika, cumin, fennel or caraway seeds
• exotic extras — Mexican style chili powder, Chinese five-spice powder, garam masala, curry paste

STOCKS

• fish, chicken, beef or vegetable in cartons or frozen, cubes (bouillon) or powder, canned consommé

SAUCES, CONDIMENTS AND DRESSINGS

• savory sauces — Worcestershire, Tabasco, ketchup (tomato sauce)
• Oriental extras — mirin or sake (substitute dry sherry), soy, hot or sweet chili, oyster
• condiments — honey, fruit chutney, marmalade, redcurrant jelly, Dijon and English mustards, gherkin relish, mint sauce, tomato salsa
• dressings — egg mayonnaise, vinegar (red or white wine, cider or malt), oil (vegetable or peanut, olive)

CANNED AND PACKAGED GOODS

• whole peeled tomatoes, tuna or salmon, condensed soups, coconut cream, tomato paste (concentrate), evaporated milk, red kidney or cannellini beans, pineapple pieces
• delicatessen delicacies — anchovy fillets, capers, marinated artichoke hearts or olives, sun-dried tomatoes

PRODUCE

• for flavoring — onions, garlic, ginger, lemons
• for salads — celery, green or red bell pepper (capsicum), scallions (shallots/spring onions), purple onion, cucumber, assorted salad leaves
• everyday standbys — tomatoes, potatoes, carrots, frozen green peas, frozen spinach

REFRIGERATED ITEMS

• milk, cream, butter, cooking margarine, eggs, cheese (including parmesan, cheddar), yogurt or sour cream, bacon

BASIC STAPLES

• flour — all-purpose (plain), self-rising (self-raising)
• sugar — granulated, superfine (caster), confectioners (icing); soft brown (light and dark)
• baking basics — leavening (baking powder, bicarbonate of soda/baking soda), cocoa powder or cooking chocolate, unsweetened shredded (desiccated) coconut, vanilla extract (essence)
• dried fruit — apricots, golden raisins (sultanas), dates
• thickeners — cornstarch (cornflour) or arrowroot
• coatings — dried breadcrumbs, soda crackers (saltines)
• cereals — bread, rice (white, brown), pasta (including elbow macaroni, spaghetti), polenta (yellow cornmeal), cracked wheat (burghul), couscous
• nuts and seeds — pine nuts, walnuts, blanched flaked almonds, sesame seeds

Poached fish

INGREDIENTS
Serves 4
1 large or 2 small whole fish, cleaned and scaled,
*   or 4 thick fillets or steaks (cutlets)*

FOR COURT BOUILLON
¹/₂ cup (4 fl oz/125 ml) white wine or orange juice
1 carrot
1 stick celery
1 lemon
1 onion, cut into quarters but not peeled
1 bay leaf
4 sprigs cilantro (fresh coriander) or parsley
¹/₂ tspn whole black peppercorns

HINTS & TIPS
• Whole fish — such as trout, salmon, perch, bream, snapper **(pictured)** — and thick fillets of any white firm-fleshed fish can be poached. Serve hot or cold.
• Suggested quantities per serving: whole, 10–12 oz (300–375 g); whole with head removed and cleaned, 7–9 oz (220–280 g); fillets, 3–5 oz (90–150 g); steaks (cutlets), 5–7 oz (150–220 g).
• Strain cooking liquid and freeze to use in soups and sauces.
• Serve fish cold garnished with sliced, unpeeled cucumbers and horseradish cream — mix 1 cup (8 fl oz/250 ml) sour cream with 1 tablespoon horseradish relish and 1 teaspoon snipped fresh chives or dill.
• Serve fish hot with hollandaise sauce (recipe page 108) and steamed whole new potatoes and other vegetables (page 42) **(pictured)**.
• Serve flaked fish as a salad with lemon herb dressing: mix 1 cup (8 fl oz/250 ml) mayonnaise (page 109) with 4 tablespoons chopped mixed fresh herbs (e.g. parsley, chives, thyme, dill) and 2 teaspoons grated lemon rind. Arrange mixture on serving plates lined with salad greens. Garnish with sliced lemon and chopped herbs.

TO MAKE
1. Trim fins and tail with kitchen shears. Rinse fish under cold running water and place in a fish poacher (fish kettle), large frying pan or heavy-based saucepan. Add wine to pan and enough cold water to barely cover fish.

2. Thickly slice carrot, celery and lemon and add to pan with onion, bay leaf, cilantro and peppercorns.

3. Cover pan, bring slowly to boil over medium heat. Reduce heat and simmer 10 minutes, or until fish is just tender when pierced with tip of a knife. Remove pan from heat and, using a slotted spoon, lift vegetables from liquid; discard. If serving fish cold, cool in liquid.

4. To prevent breaking use two spatulas to lift whole fish from liquid. Drain and transfer to a serving platter. To skin whole fish, use tip of a sharp knife to slit skin along backbone, behind the head and at the tail. Using your fingers, carefully peel off skin in strips. Turn fish and repeat.

5. To serve, carefully lift portions of flesh from one side of fish using a flat fish server. Arrange on serving plates. Lift off backbone — it should come away easily — and serve remaining portions.

Grilled, broiled or pan-fried fish

INGREDIENTS
Serves 4
4 x 6 oz (180 g) thick fish fillets or steaks (cutlets)
1–2 tbspn melted butter (for grilling or broiling)
*   or lemon juice (for pan frying)*
2 tblspn butter (for pan frying only)
lemon wedges and parsley sprigs, to garnish
*   (optional)*

FOR LEMON HERB BUTTER
2 oz (60 g) butter, softened
2 tspn finely chopped fresh dill or chives
½ tspn grated lemon rind
pinch of salt
freshly ground black pepper

HINTS & TIPS
• Any moist, white-fleshed or oily fish can be cooked
by these methods (e.g. sole, trout, perch, dory, ling flounder,
sardines, mullet, bream, tuna, salmon **(pictured)**).
• When buying fish, look for firm flesh and a pleasant
smell. Whole fish should have bright, bulging eyes, red
gills and a glossy, bright skin. Fillets or steaks should look
moist but not soggy and have no discolored or dry
patches. The bones should be firmly attached to the skin.
• To test when fish is cooked, insert a fork or the tip of
a knife into the thickest part and gently twist. If the flesh
flakes easily and is opaque, it's ready. Serve immediately.
• Coat fish for pan-frying lightly with a mixture of flour,
salt and pepper, and a pinch of spice (e.g. curry powder)
or a dried herb.
• The preparation and timing is almost the same for whole
fish. Purchase small ('plate-size') cleaned and scaled fish.
Trim fins and tail with kitchen shears. Rinse under cold
running water and dry with paper towels. If fish is thick,
use a sharp knife to slash skin in 2–3 places on each side.
Cooking time for whole fish is the same as for portions.

TO MAKE
1. To make lemon butter, mix butter, herb, rind,
salt and black pepper to taste. Transfer to a
square of foil or plastic wrap, form a log, wrap,
then refrigerate until firm.

2. Dry fish with paper towels. If fish is to be
grilled or broiled, brush with melted butter;
if pan-fried, drizzle with lemon juice.

3. **To grill, broil or barbecue:** place fish on
an oiled rack under a preheated hot broiler
(grill) or over ash-covered, glowing coals and
cook, basting occasionally with melted butter,
4–5 minutes each side or until cooked when
tested (see Hints & Tips).
To pan-fry: heat a large, heavy-based frying pan
over medium heat. Add 2 tablespoons butter
and, when foaming subsides, add fish. Cook 4–5
minutes each side or until cooked when tested.

4. Unwrap lemon herb butter and cut into thin
slices. Using a wide spatula or flat fish server,
lift fish onto heated serving plates. Place 1 or
2 slices of butter on each piece, garnish with
lemon and parsley and serve immediately.

Battered fried fish

INGREDIENTS
Serves 4

1½ lb (750 g) boneless, skinned fish fillets
    (e.g. bream, snapper, dory, perch, cod)
vegetable or peanut oil, for deep frying
lemon wedges and parsley sprigs, to serve
brown vinegar, to serve

FOR BATTER
1 egg
1 cup (8 fl oz/250 ml) chilled mineral water or
    club soda (soda water)
1 cup (4 oz/125 g) all-purpose (plain) flour

TO MAKE

1. To make batter, place egg and water in a bowl and, using a whisk, stir to combine. Sift flour into egg mixture and whisk lightly until just blended (batter should be slightly lumpy).

2. Set oven temperature to 300°F (150°C/Gas 2). Cut fish into thick strips and pat thoroughly dry with paper towels. Line a baking sheet with paper towels.

3. Pour oil into a large, heavy-based saucepan to a depth of 4 in (10 cm) and heat slowly to 350°F (180°C). Use a candy thermometer if you have one or test oil by frying a cube of bread in the oil — it should brown in 20–30 seconds.

4. Using tongs, dip fish pieces, three at a time, into batter. Gently drain off excess. Carefully lower into hot oil and deep-fry in batches, turning once, 3–5 minutes or until golden brown and crisp. Use a slotted spoon to lift out cooked pieces. Drain in a single layer on lined baking sheet.

5. Keep fish warm in oven while frying remaining pieces. Scoop out any floating pieces of batter from oil in between batches.

6. Serve with lemon, parsley and vinegar as desired.

HINTS & TIPS
• Can be served with oven-baked potato wedges (page 45) and tartare sauce, home-made (page 109) or store-bought.
• To prevent boiling over, never fill a saucepan with oil more than half-full and never use a lid when deep-frying.
• For best results, cook foods in small batches so as not to crowd the pan. Allow the oil to return to cooking temperature between each batch. If the oil begins to smoke, the temperature is too high.

Baked fish with rice stuffing

INGREDIENTS
Serves 4
4 x 5–6 oz (150–180 g) whole fish (e.g. trout, bream, snapper), cleaned and scaled
freshly ground black pepper
1 oz (30 g) butter, melted
¼ cup (2 fl oz/60 ml) lemon juice

FOR LEMON RICE STUFFING
1 cup (7 oz/220 g) white rice
½ tspn ground turmeric
¼ cup (1 oz/30 g) roughly chopped almonds or hazelnuts
2–3 tblspn chopped parsley
2–3 tspn grated lemon rind
1 egg, lightly beaten

TO MAKE
1. For stuffing, boil rice using rapid boil method (page 66), adding turmeric to water. Drain and let cool.

2. Roast nuts in a dry, nonstick frying pan over medium heat, stirring occasionally until brown. Remove from pan immediately to prevent overbrowning.

3. Combine rice and nuts in a bowl with parsley, lemon rind and egg, using a fork.

4. Preheat oven to 350°F (180°C/Gas 4). Rinse fish, inside and out, under cold running water and dry with paper towels. Sprinkle cavities lightly with black pepper and loosely fill with stuffing. Place fish, in one layer, in baking dish. Drizzle with melted butter and lemon juice.

5. Cover dish and bake 35–40 minutes, or until fish flakes easily from backbone when pierced with the tip of a knife.

HINTS & TIPS
• Most fish, whether white-fleshed or oily, whole or in fillets or steaks (cutlets) can be baked conventionally or microwaved. Whole trout are pictured.
• You can use thick fillets or steaks (cutlets) in this recipe — place the rice mixture in a baking dish, cover with a single layer of fish fillets and cook as directed.
• **To microwave:** arrange fish in one layer in a shallow, microwavable dish, with thickest parts pointing to the outside. If whole fish is thick, slash skin in 2 or 3 places with a sharp knife. Remove or pierce eyes as they can explode. Drizzle with melted butter and lemon juice. Cover and cook on MEDIUM-HIGH (70% power) 5–6 minutes per 1 lb (500 g) or until fish flakes easily. If using thicker fillets or steaks, cook on HIGH (100% power) 4–5 minutes per 1 lb (500 g). The secret to perfectly microwaved fish is to bring it to the table still cooking! Undercook fish slightly so that by the time it's served, the fish is just cooked and still quite moist.
• For a slightly sweet finish to the stuffing, add a touch of curry powder or curry paste and some chopped seedless raisins or dried apricots.

Fish stew

Preparation 10–15 minutes
Cooking time 35–40 minutes

INGREDIENTS
Serves 6
1 small leek
1 onion
2 cloves garlic
2 tblspn olive oil
14 oz (400 g) can whole, peeled tomatoes
3 cups (24 fl oz/750 ml) fish stock or water
2 tblspn each chopped fresh basil and parsley or
  1½ tspn dried
1 tblspn chopped fresh thyme or 1 tspn dried
1 bay leaf
2–3 drops hot pepper sauce, such as Tabasco
2 lb (1 kg) boneless, skinned, white-fleshed fish
  fillets (e.g. bream, snapper, ling, cod)
freshly ground black pepper
parsley sprigs, to garnish

TO MAKE
1. Remove green part of leek, halve white part lengthwise. Wash clean under cold running water, drain and slice thinly crosswise. Peel and thinly slice onion. Peel and finely chop garlic.

2. Heat oil in a large, heavy-based saucepan. Cook leek, onion and garlic over medium heat, stirring, 5 minutes or until golden.

3. Crush tomatoes and add with their juice to pan. Add stock or water, herbs, and hot pepper sauce. Bring to boil, reduce heat and simmer 25–30 minutes.

4. Cut fish into large, bite-size pieces, add to pan and simmer 5–10 minutes or until tender. Season to taste with black pepper.

5. Ladle fish and stock into wide, deep soup plates. Serve garnished with parsley.

HINTS & TIPS
• Any combination of firm white-fleshed (non-oily) fish can be used to make a simple soup-stew. Serve with a good white wine and crusty bread.
• For the look and taste of the French fish soup known as bouillabaisse, substitute ¾ cup (6 fl oz/180 ml) of the stock or water in this recipe with dry white wine and add 2–3 thin strips of orange rind (scraping off all white pith) and a pinch saffron powder or ground turmeric in Step 3.
• Packaged fish stock is available in major supermarkets. To make your own, rinse 2 lb (1 kg) fish heads and trimmings. Place in a large saucepan with court bouillon ingredients (page 10), omitting water. Simmer, stirring occasionally, until wine almost evaporates. Add 8 cups (64 fl oz/2 l) cold water and bring slowly to boil, using a slotted spoon to remove scum as it rises to surface. Reduce heat and simmer gently 20 minutes (any longer and the stock will be bitter). Strain and let cool. Freeze in small quantities.

Simple chicken sauté

Preparation 2 minutes
Cooking time 25–30 minutes

INGREDIENTS
Serves 4
4 boneless, skinned chicken breast fillets or
  2½ lb (1.25 kg) chicken, cut into 8 pieces
freshly ground black pepper
2 tblspn butter
1 tblspn vegetable or olive oil

FOR MUSTARD CREAM SAUCE
½ cup (4 fl oz/125 ml) chicken stock, dry white
  wine or water
2 tblspn Dijon mustard
1 tspn wholegrain (seeded) mustard (optional)
¾ cup (6 fl oz/180 ml) whipping cream

TO MAKE
1. Rinse chicken under cold running water and dry with paper towels. Sprinkle with pepper to taste.

2. Heat butter and oil in a large, heavy-based frying pan over medium heat. When foaming subsides, add chicken and cook 5–6 minutes on each side or until golden brown.

3. Cover pan, reduce heat and cook 8–10 minutes or until chicken is just tender — pieces on the bone take longer than fillets. Using tongs, transfer chicken to a heated serving platter and cover loosely with foil to keep warm.

4. For sauce, drain excess fat from pan, leaving 1–2 tablespoons fat with cooking juices. Add stock, mustards and cream to pan, mix well over medium heat. Bring to boil and simmer stirring occasionally, 5 minutes or until sauce reduces and thickens slightly. Pour sauce over chicken and serve immediately.

HINTS & TIPS
• **To cut up (section) a chicken:** using a sharp knife, cut skin where leg joins body, then cut through joint between thigh and body to remove leg. Cut through drumstick and thigh joint. Bend wing away from body, cut through joint, taking a small amount of breast meat with wing. Cut off wing tips. Cut through ribs on both sides of body to separate breast from back. Position breast, skin side down, and using a heavy knife or cleaver, cut breastbone in half lengthwise. If still large, cut pieces crosswise in half too. Trim off excess fat, skin and small bones from all pieces. Discard. Freeze back section and wing tips for stock.
• **For a mushroom sauce:** slice 4 oz (125 g) button mushrooms and cook with chicken in Step 3. Use chicken stock instead of wine or water and substitute 2 tablespoons dry sherry for mustard.

Crispy chicken

Preparation 5 minutes
Cooking time 35–40 minutes, oven fried
Cooking time 10–15 minutes, pan-fried
Refrigeration time 20 minutes

INGREDIENTS
Serves 4
4 skinned, boned chicken breast halves or thighs
1/4 cup (1 oz/30 g) flour
salt and freshly ground black pepper
1 egg
1 tblspn milk
1 cup (4 oz/125 g) dried breadcrumbs
2 tblspn butter, for pan-frying
2 tblspn vegetable oil, for pan-frying

TO MAKE
1. Rinse and dry chicken with paper towels.

2. Place flour in a plastic bag. Season with salt and pepper; shake to mix. Spread onto a shallow dish. Place egg and milk in another shallow dish and, using a fork, beat to combine. Place breadcrumbs on a third dish.

3. Using tongs, coat chicken on both sides in flour, dip into egg then press into breadcrumbs to coat evenly. Place on a plate lined with greaseproof (waxed) paper, and refrigerate 20 minutes to set coating.

4. **To oven-fry:** preheat oven to 350°F (180°C/Gas 4). Place chicken in a lightly greased baking dish, cover and bake 15 minutes. Turn chicken over, re-cover and bake 10 minutes. Remove cover and bake 10–15 minutes, or until cooked and golden.
To pan-fry: heat butter and oil in a large, heavy-based frying pan over medium heat until butter stops foaming. Add chicken and cook 5–8 minutes each side or until tender and golden. Serve.

HINTS & TIPS
• Powdered herbs and spices can be added to the flour. Try a pinch of cayenne pepper, paprika, ground cumin, curry powder, dried sage, oregano or dill, or finely grated lemon rind.
• **To make homemade dried breadcrumbs:** place 4 slices white sandwich bread on a baking sheet and bake at 300°F (150°C/Gas 2), turning occasionally, for 12–15 minutes or until dry and golden. Let cool then process in a blender or food processor until finely crumbed. Store in an airtight container.
• Instead of chicken, use 1 1/2 lb (750 g) veal schnitzel, 4 x 6 oz (180 g) boneless thick white-fleshed fish fillets or 8 trimmed lamb rib chops (cutlets). If using fish, rinse and dry with paper towels. Crumb and chill as directed in Step 3.
To oven-fry: bake as directed in Step 4 except reduce time to 8–10 minutes each side plus 8–10 minutes uncovered.
To pan-fry: cook as directed in Step 4 except reduce time to 4–5 minutes each side or until cooked.

Roast chicken with lemon herb stuffing

INGREDIENTS
Serves 4
3 lb (1.5kg) roasting chicken
salt
2 tblspn melted butter
½ cup (4 fl oz/125 ml) cold water

FOR STUFFING
6 slices white bread
1 onion, peeled
2 scallions (spring onions/shallots)
4 sprigs fresh parsley, leaves only
4–6 fresh sage leaves or ½ tspn ground
2 tspn finely grated lemon rind
¼ tspn freshly ground black pepper
1 egg
2 tblspn melted butter
2–3 tbspns water

TO MAKE
1. Preheat oven to 375°F (190°C/Gas 5). Remove neck and giblets from chicken (if present) and reserve for making gravy. Rinse chicken under cold running water, drain and pat dry thoroughly with paper towels.

2. To make stuffing, remove crusts from bread, cut into cubes, and process in food processor until crumbed — do this in batches. Transfer to bowl. Roughly chop onion and scallions and process with parsley and sage until finely chopped. Transfer to bowl with crumbs. Add lemon rind, black pepper, egg and butter and mix lightly with fork, adding enough water to make a moist mixture.

3. Sprinkle cavity of chicken with a little salt and loosely fill with stuffing. Fold skin flap at neck opening under body and secure it by folding wings behind back. Using kitchen string, tie wings together then legs together and then tie to tail so they lay snugly against the body.

4. Place chicken, breast side down, on a rack in a roasting pan and brush all over with butter. Pour ½ cup water into pan. Roast 60 minutes. Begin making gravy (see page 108).

5. Turn chicken over and roast 45–60 minutes more or until chicken is cooked, occasionally spooning cooking juices over.

6. Transfer chicken to a warm serving platter, remove strings. Cover chicken loosely with foil while finishing gravy. Serve with warm gravy and vegetables.

HINTS & TIPS
• Serve with chicken gravy (page 108), mashed potatoes and steamed fresh vegetables (page 42).
• To test when cooked, pierce thickest part of thigh with a skewer. If juices run clear chicken is ready; if still pink, roast 15–20 more minutes and test again.

Curried chicken casserole

Preparation 10 minutes
Cooking time 35–45 minutes

INGREDIENTS
Serves 4–6
3 lb (1.5 kg) chicken, cut into pieces (page 20)
1/4 cup (1 oz/30 g) all-purpose (plain) flour
3/4 tspn salt
1/4 tspn freshly ground black pepper
1/4 tspn paprika
1 clove garlic
1 small onion
1 small green bell pepper (capsicum)
2 oz (60 g) butter
2 tspn curry powder or curry paste
1/2 tspn dried thyme
14 oz (400 g) can whole, peeled tomatoes,
    undrained and crushed
3 tblspn dried currants or chopped seedless raisins
3 tblspn chopped fresh parsley or cilantro
    (coriander leaves)
1/4 cup sliced almonds
cooked rice or couscous (page 64–66 or 72), to serve
fruit chutney, to serve

TO MAKE
1. Rinse chicken pieces under cold running water and dry with paper towels.

2. Place flour, salt, pepper and paprika in a plastic bag, or container. Place 1 or 2 chicken pieces at a time into bag, seal and shake to coat.

3. Peel and finely chop garlic and onion. Halve bell pepper, remove seeds and cut into 1/4 in (5 mm) squares.

4. Melt butter in a large, heavy-based frying pan over medium heat until foaming subsides. Add chicken, in batches, cook 1–2 minutes each side or until brown. Transfer cooked chicken to a plate. Drain excess fat from pan, leaving 1–2 tablespoons fat with cooking juices.

5. Add garlic, onion and pepper to pan and cook, stirring, over medium heat 3–5 minutes or until onion is golden. Add remaining ingredients except chicken and almonds and bring to boil.

6. Return chicken to pan and cover. Reduce heat and simmer gently 20–30 minutes or until chicken is tender.

7. Just before serving, roast almonds (step 2, page 16). Serve chicken on rice or couscous, sprinkled with almonds and accompanied by fruit chutney.

HINTS & TIPS
• **To casserole chicken:** use a flameproof casserole dish in Step 4 and proceed as directed to end of Step 5. Bake in a preheated oven at 375°F (190°C/Gas 5), 45–50 minutes, or until chicken is tender. Remove lid during last 10 minutes to reduce cooking liquids.
• **To microwave:** prepare recipe as directed to end of Step 4. Place chicken in a microwavable dish with meatiest parts to outer edges. Proceed with step 5 and pour mixture over chicken. Cover and cook on MEDIUM-HIGH (70%) 5 minutes. Turn chicken over, cover and cook on MEDIUM (50%) 5–6 minutes. Let stand 3 minutes before serving.

Traditional roast beef

Preparation 5–10 minutes
Cooking time 1¾–2 hours

INGREDIENTS
Serves 6
3–4 lb (1.5–1.75 kg) beef for roasting e.g. rump,
*   loin, sirloin or rib (pictured)*
3 onions
1 bay leaf, crumbled
1 tspn peeled and finely chopped garlic
1 tspn freshly ground black pepper
1 cup (8 fl oz/250 ml) water
6 carrots
6 potatoes
pan gravy (page 108) (optional)

TO MAKE
1. Preheat oven to 350°F (180°C/Gas 4). Place roast on a rack in large roasting pan. Peel and quarter onions and arrange under rack. Combine bay leaf, garlic and pepper and rub over meat. Add water to pan under rack. Cover with lid or foil and roast 45 minutes.

2. Peel and cut carrots and potatoes into large pieces of equal size. Add to roasting pan and baste with cooking juices. Roast, basting meat occasionally, 60–65 minutes more, or until vegetables are tender and meat is cooked to your liking.

3. Transfer meat and vegetables to a heated serving platter, cover with foil and let stand 10 minutes in a warm place to settle juices before carving.

4. Prepare pan gravy, if using, or serve meat and vegetables with cooking juices.

HINTS & TIPS
• **To roast lamb:** place a 3 lb (1.5 kg) leg of lamb, fat side up, in a roasting pan. Combine 2 cloves finely chopped garlic, 2 teaspoons crushed fresh or 1 teaspoon dried rosemary leaves, and ½ teaspoon freshly ground black pepper. Rub over lamb. Roast, uncovered, at 350°F (180°C/Gas 4), 1–2 hours. Serve with pan-roasted vegetables (page 44), green peas or asparagus, mint jelly or mint sauce (page 109). Refer to roasting guide (page 5).

Herb-marinated roast pork

Preparation 5–10 minutes
Cooking time 1½–1¾ hours
Refrigeration time 4–6 hours

INGREDIENTS
Serves 6

3 lb (1.5 kg) boneless loin of pork or shoulder roast,
    rind removed, rolled and tied
1 onion
1 clove garlic
3–4 sprigs fresh sage or ½ tspn dried
3 sprigs fresh thyme or ½ tspn dried
1 bay leaf, crushed
4 whole cloves
1½ cups (12 fl oz/375 ml) unsweetened
    apple cider, white wine or beer
2 tblspn olive oil
freshly ground black pepper
pan gravy (page 108) (optional)

TO MAKE

1. Place pork in a plastic bag and set in a shallow dish.

2. Peel and slice onion and garlic; place in a bowl. Add herbs, cloves, cider and oil, mix well and pour into bag with pork. Seal and refrigerate, 4–6 hours, turning occasionally.

3. Preheat oven to 350°F (180°C/Gas 4). Drain pork, reserving marinade, and dry with paper towels. Place in a roasting pan with ½ cup (4 fl oz/125 ml) marinade and roast, basting occasionally, 1½–1¾ hours, or until juices run clear when thickest part of meat is pierced with a skewer — a meat thermometer should register 170°F (76°C).

4. Transfer roast to a heated serving platter and sprinkle with pepper to taste. Cover with foil. Let stand in a warm place 10 minutes to settle juices before carving.

5. Make pan gravy, if using. Slice pork thinly and serve with gravy.

HINTS & TIPS

• **To make crackling (pictured)**: reserve pork rind and cook separately from meat. Score rind, rub well with salt and cut into strips or short pieces. Place in a baking dish. While roast is standing increase oven temperature to 425°F (220°C/Gas 7) and roast rind until puffed and crisp, about 20–25 minutes.
• **To microwave rind**, place in shallow dish between several thicknesses of paper towels and cook on HIGH (100%) 5–6 minutes, moving around occasionally so that center pieces don't burn. Serve with pork.
• **To make baked apple accompaniment (pictured)**: peel, core and halve 3 Granny Smith, Golden Delicious or Rome Beauty apples and add to dish, cut side down, 40 minutes before meat is cooked. Roast 20 minutes. Turn apples, baste and fill centers with 1 teaspoon redcurrant jelly or cranberry sauce. Continue roasting until pork and apples are tender, about 20 minutes more.

Perfectly cooked steaks

INGREDIENTS
Serves 4
4 x 6–8 oz (180–250 g) steaks e.g. T-bone, sirloin,
*   porterhouse, rib-eye (scotch) fillet, new york strip,*
*   (pictured) cut 1-in (2.5 cm) thick*
vegetable or olive oil
freshly ground black pepper

TO MAKE
1. Heat barbecue until coals are ash-covered and glowing, or preheat a broiler (grill) to medium-high. Place cooking rack about 4 in (10 cm) away from heat.

2. Trim excess fat from steaks and sprinkle with black pepper to taste. Brush rack with oil to prevent meat sticking.

3. Cook steaks 30–45 seconds each side. Reduce heat slightly (or move steaks from hot part of barbecue) and cook, turning once only, 4–5 minutes each side or until cooked as desired. Serve immediately.

HINTS & TIPS
• Whether barbecued, grilled or broiled, the rule is the same: sear meat quickly on both sides to seal in juices, reduce heat and cook as desired. This also applies to chops, whether lamb, pork or veal.
• **To test if cooked:** press the meat with tongs — never cut or pierce with a knife or fork as juices will run and meat will be dry. Rare steak feels soft and red juices puddle on the surface; medium is firm but pliable and juices are still pink; well-done is firm, stiff and dry-looking.
• Marinate steak 30–60 minutes at room temperature in ½ cup (4 fl oz/125 ml) beer, 1 clove garlic (peeled and finely chopped), and 1 tablespoon each hot English mustard and honey. Drain steaks, reserving marinade, and pat dry with paper towels. Cook, basting once or twice with marinade.
• Rub steak with olive oil and sprinkle with crumbled dried rosemary, thyme, oregano or sage leaves.
• Serve steaks with a savory butter. Beat 4 oz (125 g) soft butter until creamy with one or more of the following: 1–2 tablespoons hot English mustard, horseradish relish or chili sauce; 2–3 teaspoons grated lemon rind; 2 peeled and finely chopped garlic cloves; 2–3 tablespoons chopped fresh herb (or 1–2 teaspoons dried) such as mint, basil, sage, rosemary, dill, chives, or a combination.

Braised chops

INGREDIENTS
Serves 4
1¼–1½ lb (625–750 g) lamb, veal or pork chops
 (pictured) from shoulder blade, forequarter,
 best neck, arm or leg (chump)
freshly ground black pepper
2 tblspn vegetable or olive oil or butter
1 small onion
1 small stalk celery
¾ cup (6 fl oz/180 ml) liquid (see below)
½ tspn dried herb such as thyme, sage, rosemary
1 tblspn cornstarch (cornflour)
2 tblspn cold water
salt
2–3 tblspn chopped parsley, to garnish (optional)

HINTS & TIPS
• The cuts of meat listed above are not very tender and so
benefit from the long cooking time. For best results, the
chops should be about ¾–1 in (2–2.5 cm) thick.
• For liquid, use water, stock, dry white or red wine,
unsweetened fruit juice e.g. orange or pineapple or apricot
nectar, or undrained crushed canned tomatoes.
• Chopped scallions (shallots/spring onions), sliced leek
or garlic, sliced button mushrooms or finely diced carrots
can be added in Step 3.
• Variations in Step 4 can include: *for pork* — 6–8 dried
apricots or pitted prunes, 1 peeled, cored and sliced tart
cooking apple; *for lamb* — 2 teaspoons curry paste, strips
of orange or lemon rind; *for veal* — chopped fresh dill
or chives, 1 teaspoon paprika, squeeze of lemon juice.
• Tender pork, lamb and veal chops cut from the rib or
loin can also be barbecued, grilled, broiled or pan-broiled
(pan-grilled). See page 32.

TO MAKE
1. Preheat oven to lowest temperature. Trim
excess fat from chops. Slash remaining fat
almost through to meat in several places, to
prevent curling. Sprinkle with pepper to taste.

2. Heat oil in a large, heavy-based frying pan
over medium heat. Add chops and cook
2–3 minutes each side, or until brown. Transfer
chops to a plate and keep warm. Drain excess
fat from pan, leaving 1–2 tablespoons fat with
cooking juices.

3. Peel and chop onion and thinly slice celery.
Add to pan and cook over medium heat,
stirring, 5 minutes or until golden. Add liquid
and herb to pan and bring to a boil.

4. Return chops to pan, reduce heat, cover and
simmer gently 20–25 minutes or until tender,
turning chops once. Less tender cuts may take
5–10 minutes more. Transfer chops to heated
serving plate and keep warm in oven.

5. Mix cornstarch and water until blended.
Add to cooking juices. Cook, stirring
constantly until sauce boils and thickens.
Season to taste with salt and pepper.

6. Pour sauce over chops, sprinkle with parsley
and serve immediately.

One-pot meals

INGREDIENTS
Serves 4
1½ lb (750 g) boneless lean beef, pork or lamb
2 tblspn all-purpose (plain) flour
salt and freshly ground black pepper
2 tblspn vegetable or olive oil
1 oz (30 g) butter
1 large onion
2 cups (16 fl oz/500 ml) liquid (see below)
12 oz (375 g) vegetables or fruit (see below)
seasonings (see below)
extras (see below)
cooked rice, pasta or couscous
  (pages 64–66 and 72), to serve

TO MAKE
1. Use a sharp knife to trim excess fat from meat. Cut into 1-in (2.5 cm) cubes.

2. Place flour and salt and pepper to taste in a plastic bag. Add meat, seal and shake until cubes are evenly coated.

3. Heat oil and butter in a deep, heavy-based frying pan over medium heat until foaming subsides. Add meat in batches and cook, turning frequently, until brown on all sides. Use a slotted spoon to transfer meat to a plate as it cooks.

4. Peel and chop onion, add to pan and cook, stirring, over medium heat 5 minutes or until soft. Return meat to pan with liquid, vegetables or fruit and seasonings and bring to boil, stirring. Reduce heat, partially cover and simmer 1 hour or until meat is almost tender, stirring occasionally.

5. Add extras to pan and simmer, uncovered, 15–20 minutes until meat is tender and sauce thickens slightly. Serve with cooked rice, pasta or couscous.

HINTS & TIPS
• **Pork Provençal:** For liquid, use 14 oz (400 g) canned tomatoes with their juice and 1 cup (8 fl oz/250 ml) chicken or beef stock. For vegetables, add 2 chopped stalks celery and 4–6 sliced scallions (spring onions/shallots). For seasonings, add 1 teaspoon fennel seeds. For extras, use 2 peeled and segmented oranges and ½ cup (2 oz/60 g) coarsely chopped walnuts. Serve with noodles.
• **Beef Morocco:** For liquid, use beef stock. For fruit, add 1 cup (5 oz/150 g) each pitted prunes and dried apricot halves. For seasonings, add 1 teaspoon each ground cinnamon and ginger. For extras, add ½ cup (2 oz/60 g) toasted blanched whole almonds. Serve with rice or couscous and steamed vegetables.
• **Irish Lamb Pot (pictured):** sauté 4 oz (125 g) chopped bacon with onion in Step 4. For liquid, use beef stock. For vegetables, add 2 peeled and thickly sliced carrots, 8 peeled and halved small onions and 6 oz (180 g) halved button mushrooms. For seasonings, use 1 teaspoon dried thyme or marjoram. For extras, stir in ½ cup (2 oz/60 g) frozen peas. Serve with rice.

Savory beef

Preparation 5 minutes
Cooking time 35–45 minutes

INGREDIENTS
Bolognese Sauce for 4
$^1/_2$ stick celery
1 onion
1 clove garlic
2 tblspn olive or vegetable oil
12 oz (375 g) lean ground (minced) beef
2 x 14 oz (400 g) cans whole peeled tomatoes
2 tblspn tomato paste (concentrate)
3–4 tblspn chopped fresh parsley
2 tblspn chopped fresh oregano or 1 tspn dried
1 tblspn chopped fresh basil or $^1/_2$ tspn dried
$^1/_4$ tspn ground nutmeg
pinch of sugar
salt and freshly ground black pepper

TO MAKE
1. Trim coarse ends from celery and finely chop. Peel and finely chop onion and garlic.

2. Heat oil in a large, heavy-based saucepan over medium heat and cook celery, onion and garlic, stirring, 5 minutes or until golden.

3. Crumble beef into pan and cook until brown, stirring to break up lumps.

4. Add undrained, crushed tomatoes, and remaining ingredients. Bring to boil. Reduce heat and simmer gently, stirring occasionally, 30–40 minutes or until sauce thickens. Serve over cooked pasta.

HINTS & TIPS
• Add 2 tablespoons grated parmesan cheese and $^1/_4$ teaspoon fennel seeds to sauce in Step 4.
Slice 6–8 button mushrooms, sauté in a little butter, and stir in before serving.
• **For Chili con Carne (pictured):** omit parsley, basil and nutmeg. Step 2. Halve, seed and wash 1 green bell pepper (capsicum), cut into $^1/_2$ in (1 cm) squares and cook with vegetables. Step 4. Increase oregano to 3 tablespoons fresh or 1 tablespoon dried and add 1$^1/_2$ tablespoons ground cumin and 2 teaspoons Mexican-style chili powder.
Rinse a 14 oz (400 g) can red kidney beans under cold running water, drain and add to chili 10 minutes before end of cooking time. Serve over rice or elbow macaroni.
• **For Cottage Pie:** omit tomatoes, tomato paste and nutmeg in Step 4. Add $^3/_4$ cup (6 fl oz/180 ml) beef stock or dry red wine, simmer as directed, then stir in 1$^1/_2$ tablespoons all-purpose (plain) flour. Transfer to a 4 cup (32 fl oz/1 litre) shallow ovenproof dish and top with mashed potatoes (page 44), using a fork to spread potato to edges. Brush with a little melted butter. Bake in preheated oven at 350°F (180°C/Gas 4) until potatoes are brown, about 25–30 minutes.

Best burgers

INGREDIENTS
Serves 6
$\frac{1}{2}$ small onion
1 clove garlic (optional)
1–2 sprigs fresh parsley, leaves only
2 tspn chopped fresh sage or $\frac{1}{2}$ tspn dried
$\frac{3}{4}$ tspn salt
$\frac{1}{4}$ tspn freshly ground black pepper
pinch nutmeg (optional)
$1\frac{1}{2}$ lb (750 g) lean ground (minced) meat
   e.g. beef, pork or veal, or a combination
2 tblspn vegetable oil or butter
6 hamburger breadrolls
6 leaves lettuce
6 slices tomato
ketchup (tomato sauce) and mustard, to serve

TO MAKE
1. Peel and finely chop onion and garlic and chop parsley. Combine with sage, salt, black pepper and nutmeg in a large bowl. Add meat and, using wet hands, mix thoroughly.

2. Divide mixture into six portions and shape into patties about $\frac{3}{4}$ in (1.5 cm) thick. Place on a plate lined with waxed (greaseproof) paper and refrigerate 15 minutes.

3. Heat oil or butter in a large, heavy-based frying pan over medium heat. Add patties and cook 5–6 minutes each side, turning once only, or until cooked through and brown.

4. Split and toast breadrolls. Top with burgers, lettuce, tomato, ketchup and mustard. Serve immediately.

HINTS & TIPS
• To toast breadrolls, place halves, cut side up, under a preheated medium broiler (grill) and cook until golden.
• Burger mixture can be shaped just as easily into a meatloaf.
• **To make Glazed Meatloaf:** preheat oven to 350°F (180°C/Gas 4). Whisk together 2 eggs, $\frac{3}{4}$ cup (6 fl oz/180 ml) milk and $\frac{1}{2}$ cup (2 oz/60 g) dried breadcrumbs in a mixing bowl. Add burger ingredients and, using wet hands, mix thoroughly. Shape mixture into a thick rectangle in center of a shallow baking dish. Bake, uncovered, 45 minutes. Mix $\frac{1}{3}$ cup (3 fl oz/90 ml) ketchup, 2 tablespoons soft brown sugar and 1 tablespoon prepared mild mustard and spread over meatloaf. Bake 15 minutes more or until loaf is firm, top is glazed and juices run clear when loaf is pierced in center.

VEGETABLE SERVING GUIDE

• As a general rule, 12–16 oz (375–500 g) prepared raw vegetables will serve 4 as a side dish after cooking.

• Serve cooked vegetables drizzled with lemon juice, melted butter or warmed honey; sprinkled with toasted almonds or pine nuts, grated parmesan cheese, chopped fresh herbs e.g. mint, dill, chives or parsley; or with yogurt, white sauce or cheese sauce (page 109) spooned over.

GENERAL PREPARATION

• Dense vegetables such as carrots or green beans take longer to cook than vegetables with a higher water content, e.g. scallions (spring onions/ shallots), snow peas (mange tout), or mushrooms. When cooking a combination, begin with dense vegetables, then add those requiring less cooking, so that all vegetables are ready at the same time.

TO STEAM VEGETABLES

• **For leafy greens such as English spinach, swiss chard (silverbeet) and bok choy:** Rinse in running water. Drain briefly and place in a heavy-based saucepan, cover tightly and cook over medium heat, stirring occasionally, 2–3 minutes until tender and wilted. Drain well.

• **Other vegetables:** prepare and place in a collapsible metal steamer insert or metal or bamboo steamer basket. Place over 1–2 in (2.5–5 cm) simmering water in a saucepan — water should not touch vegetables. Cover tightly and steam until tender, 5–10 minutes depending on vegetable.

• **Combinations include:** cabbage, carrots, new potatoes, sliced onion, and a sprinkling of fennel or caraway seeds; cauliflower and broccoli florets with sliced scallions (spring onions/shallots) and dill; shelled peas and a mint sprig.

TO STIR-FRY VEGETABLES

• Cut vegetables into bite-size pieces. Use a wok or deep, heavy-based frying pan with sloping sides. Heat pan over high heat, add 1–2 tablespoons vegetable oil and swirl pan to coat base and sides. Add vegetables in stages, according to density, and using a spoon or spatula, stir and turn vegetables until just tender — they should still be slightly crisp. Serve immediately.

• **Flavorings and seasonings for stir-fried vegetables:** soy sauce, dry sherry or sake; black bean, oyster or sweet chili sauce; sesame seeds; toasted pine nuts, cashew nuts or peanuts; fresh herbs e.g. cilantro (coriander), parsley, chives or basil.

TO MICROWAVE VEGETABLES

• Use a shallow microwavable serving dish that will hold vegetables snugly. Alternatively, wrap bundles of vegetables in microwavable plastic wrap, oven bags or freezer bags (without metal ties), piercing holes for steam, and cook on a microwavable plate.

1. Cut vegetables into uniform pieces and arrange in container with large, firm vegetables or those low in moisture around outside and small or high-moisture vegetables in center; place unevenly-shaped pieces in container so that the denser or thickest parts are nearest the edge.

2. Add 1–2 tablespoons water (fruit juice, stock) to container with dense or low-moisture vegetables (this is not necessary with vegetables of high moisture content). To prevent toughening, add salt after cooking.

3. Cover container with lid or plastic wrap. Cook on HIGH (100%), stirring or rearranging once or twice, as directed by manufacturer. Serve immediately.

TO BOIL VEGETABLES

• **To boil vegetables, except potatoes:** place prepared vegetable in a saucepan with enough boiling salted water to barely cover. Cover pan and simmer until just tender when pierced with a skewer, about 5–12 minutes depending on vegetable. Drain well.

• To boil potatoes, see page 56.

• Try cooking vegetables in stock rather than water, then reserve cooking liquid for use in soups and sauces.

• **To mash or puree roots and tubers** — e.g. potato, yam (red sweet potato), turnip, rutabaga/ yellow turnip (swede), parsnip and carrot, and winter squash or pumpkin: boil as directed above. Drain, reserving $1/2$ cup (4 fl oz/ 125 ml) cooking water (or use hot milk or stock). Return hot vegetable to pan, add reserved liquid 1–2 tablespoons butter and seasonings to taste. Mash with a fork or hand-held masher, or puree in a food processor for a smooth consistency.

TO BRAISE VEGETABLES

1. Winter vegetables such as leeks, fennel, carrots, parsnips, cabbage or Brussels sprouts braise well. Trim and halve leeks, carrots or parsnips, cut cabbage into 2–3 in (5–7.5 cm)-thick wedges; halve sprouts or cut a cross in bases and leave whole.
2. Cook gently with chopped onion in a little butter or olive oil, in a heavy-based frying pan, over medium heat 5 minutes, or until onion is soft. Add $1/4$–$1/3$ cup (2–3 fl oz/60–90 ml) stock or water (or a mixture of wine or fruit juice and water) and cover. Simmer until vegetable is just tender. Season to taste with salt, black pepper, herbs or seasonings.

• Flavorings can include honey, balsamic or herbed vinegar, garlic, sliced fresh chilies, sautéed sliced almonds or diced dried fruits.

TO BAKE VEGETABLES

1. Preheat oven to 400°F (200°C/Gas 6).
2. **To bake whole vegetables** — e.g. potatoes, yams (red sweet potatoes), beets: scrub to remove grit, dry with paper towels and rub all over with oiled hands. (Do not peel beets until after baking.) Place directly on oven shelf and bake 45–60 minutes or until tender when pierced with a skewer.

• **For pan-roasted vegetables** — e.g. pumpkin, onion, new potatoes, carrots: cut 2 oz (60 g) butter into small pieces and scatter in an ovenproof dish. Place vegetables in dish, sprinkle with black pepper and a dried herb. Add 2–3 tablespoons water or stock to dish, cover and bake 20 minutes. Turn vegetables, cover and bake 10–15 minutes more or until tender.

Potato wedges

Preparation 10 minutes
Cooking time 30–40 minutes

INGREDIENTS
Serves 2–4
4 medium baking potatoes
2–3 tablespoons vegetable or olive oil
salt
chopped fresh chives or parsley, to serve (optional)
sour cream, to serve (optional)

TO MAKE

1. Preheat oven to 400°F (200°C/Gas 6). Scrub baking potatoes. Cut lengthwise into thin wedges. Pat dry with paper towels.

2. Place potatoes in a bowl. Add oil and sprinkle with coarse sea salt. Toss lightly to coat potatoes well with oil.

3. Spread in a single layer on a baking sheet. Bake on lower shelf, 30–40 minutes or until cooked and golden, turning potatoes once or twice.

4. If desired, sprinkle with chopped chives or parsley. Serve hot with a bowl of sour cream for dipping.

HINTS & TIPS
• Potatoes can also be peeled and cut into traditional sticks to make oven-baked French fries.
• Use coarsely ground sea salt for the best flavor.
• Serve as an accompaniment to meat and fish dishes such as steaks (page 32) and battered fried fish (page 14).

Sesame stir-fried green vegetables

INGREDIENTS
Serves 4

1 in (2.5cm) piece fresh ginger
2 cloves garlic
6 scallions (spring onions/shallots)
2 sticks celery
8–10 asparagus spears, green beans or snow peas
    (mange tout), or a combination
2 medium unpeeled zucchini (courgettes)
8 oyster mushrooms, optional
6 oz (180 g) English spinach or young Swiss chard
    (silverbeet) leaves
1 tblspn sesame seeds
2 tblspn vegetable or peanut oil
$\frac{1}{2}$ tspn sesame oil
1 tblspn dry sherry
1 tblspn soy sauce, preferably light

TO MAKE

1. Prepare vegetables. With a small vegetable knife, peel ginger, slice thinly then cut into slivers. Peel garlic and slice thinly. Trim coarse green tops from scallions, leaving about 1 in (2.5 cm) of tender green attached. Cut lengthwise in half. Cut celery into long diagonal slices. Trim tough ends from asparagus, and stalk ends from green beans or snow peas. Cut into 2-3 in (5–7.5 cm) lengths or leave whole. Cut zucchini into sticks of the same size. Leave mushrooms whole. Rinse spinach and remove any coarse stems.

2. Toast sesame seeds by placing in a small, dry nonstick frying pan over medium heat. Stir frequently until golden. Remove immediately from pan to prevent overbrowning and let cool.

3. Place a wok or deep, heavy-based frying pan with sloping sides over high heat. When hot, add oils and swirl pan to coat sides. Add ginger, garlic and scallions to pan and stir-fry 30 seconds.

4. Add celery, asparagus and zucchini. Stir-fry 3–5 minutes or until bright green and almost tender.

5. Add mushrooms, spinach, sherry and soy sauce and stir-fry until leaves are wilted and vegetables are cooked to your liking (they should be tender but still crisp).

6. Sprinkle with sesame seeds and serve immediately.

HINTS & TIPS
• Serve with brown rice, Chinese noodles or couscous (see pages 64–66 and 72).
• For even cooking, cut vegetables into same-size pieces.
• For authenticity, substitute sake or mirin (the latter is sweeter) for sherry. Both these rice wines are available at specialist food stores and major supermarkets.

Vegetable curry

INGREDIENTS
Serves 4–6
8 oz (250 g) cauliflower
8 oz (250 g) broccoli
2 carrots or young parsnips
3–4 finger-thick eggplant (aubergines) or unpeeled
  zucchini (courgettes)
4 oz (125 g) button mushrooms
6 oz (180 g) green beans or $^{1}/_{2}$ cup (2 oz/60 g)
  shelled fresh or frozen peas
1 large onion
2 cloves garlic
$^{1}/_{2}$ in (1 cm) piece green ginger
2 tblspn vegetable oil
1 tblspn curry paste
1 tspn chopped fresh red chilies
14 oz (400 g) can whole peeled tomatoes
$1^{1}/_{2}$ cups (12 fl oz/375 ml) water or vegetable stock
2–3 tblspn chopped fresh cilantro (coriander)
  (optional)

TO MAKE
1. Prepare vegetables: cut cauliflower and broccoli into florets. Peel and thickly slice carrots or parsnips. Trim ends from eggplant or zucchini then halve or quarter lengthwise; salt eggplant to degorge juices (page 4). Halve or quarter mushrooms. Trim beans and cut into 2–3 in (5–7.5 cm) lengths. Set aside.

2. Peel onion and garlic and finely chop. Use a sharp knife to peel ginger; thinly slice then cut into thin strips.

3. Heat oil in a large, heavy-based saucepan over medium heat. Add onion, garlic, ginger, curry paste and chili and cook, stirring, 5 minutes or until onion is soft. Add vegetables and cook, stirring, 5 minutes.

4. Add undrained, crushed tomatoes and water to pan and bring to boil. Reduce heat and simmer gently, stirring occasionally, 15 minutes or until vegetables are tender but still crisp.

5. Sprinkle with cilantro and serve.

HINTS & TIPS
• Serve as part of an Indian curry feast with other meat dishes, as an accompaniment to grilled steak, chicken or fish, or with rice (page 64–66), couscous (page 72) or pappadums **(pictured)** as a vegetarian-style meal. Vary the vegetables to suit your taste and seasonal availability.
• There are a number of commercially prepared curry pastes available from international sections in major supermarkets and oriental food stores. Experiment with them as they vary in flavor and intensity.
• Other suitable vegetables include: peeled and cubed yams (red sweet potatoes) or butternut squash (pumpkin); thickly sliced leek; fresh or frozen broad (fava) beans or lima beans; small squash.
• Use thick canned coconut milk instead of water or stock to make a slightly creamy, coconut version.
• Add $^{1}/_{2}$ cup (4 oz/125 ml) rinsed and drained canned chickpeas (garbanzo beans), red kidney beans or cannellini beans to heat through just before serving.

Chunky vegetable soup

Preparation 10 minutes
Cooking time 25–30 minutes

INGREDIENTS
Serves 4–6
2 large onions
2 cloves garlic
1 stick celery
1 tblspn olive oil
3 cups (24 fl oz/750 ml) tomato or mixed
    vegetable juice
3 cups (24 fl oz/750 ml) chicken or vegetable stock
6 unpeeled small new potatoes
8 oz (250 g) young turnips
1 lb (500 g) carrots or young parsnips
    — or a combination
4 unpeeled zucchini (courgettes)
6–8 small yellow squash
½ cup (2 oz/60 g) frozen peas or whole corn kernels
2–3 sprigs fresh parsley, chopped
2 tblspn chopped fresh basil or 1 tspn dried
freshly ground black pepper
crusty bread, to serve

TO MAKE
1. Peel and chop onion and garlic. Trim and chop celery. Heat oil in a large, heavy-based saucepan over medium heat and cook onion, garlic and celery, stirring, 5 minutes or until golden. Add juice and stock to pan and bring to boil.

2. Cut potatoes and turnips into 1 in (2.5 cm) chunks and add to pan. Reduce heat and simmer 12–15 minutes, or until vegetables are almost tender.

3. Meanwhile, peel and dice carrots or parsnips into ½ in (1 cm) cubes. Trim ends from zucchini, halve or quarter lengthwise and thickly slice. Halve and thickly slice squash.

4. Add to pan with peas, parsley, basil and pepper to taste. Simmer, stirring occasionally, 10 minutes or until vegetables are tender.

5. Serve in heated deep soup plates with crusty bread.

HINTS & TIPS
• Any fresh or dried herb such as dill, chives, tarragon or oregano can be substituted for basil. Add ½ teaspoon fennel or caraway seeds for fragrance and flavor.
• **To make minestrone:** add ⅓ cup (1½ oz /45 g) tiny pasta shapes or 2–3 tblspn rice in Step 4 and cook until tender. Just before serving, stir in 1¼ cups (10 oz/300 g) rinsed and drained canned chickpeas (garbanzo beans), cannellini beans or red kidney beans and heat through. Serve soup sprinkled with chopped fresh parsley and shaved parmesan (use a swivel-bladed vegetable peeler to shave strips off a large piece of room-temperature cheese).
• **To make chicken stock:** place 2 lb (1 kg) chicken backs, necks and wing tips in a large heavy-based saucepan with 2 broken celery sticks and tops, 1 large quartered unpeeled onion, 1 sliced carrot, 1 teaspoon salt, 5 black peppercorns and 8 cups (64 fl oz/2 litres) cold water. Bring slowly to boil, reduce heat, partly cover and simmer gently 1 hour. Strain, discarding solids. Makes about 6 cups (48 fl oz/1.5 litres).
• **Serve soup with grilled cheese toast (pictured):** cut a French bread stick into ½ in (1 cm)-thick slices and place in one layer on a baking sheet. Toast under a medium-hot broiler (grill) until golden on one side. Turn bread, brush lightly with melted butter and rub with a cut clove of garlic. Sprinkle with grated parmesan or mozzarella cheese and toast until cheese melts. Serve hot.

Ratatouille

Preparation 50 minutes
Cooking time 25–30 minutes

INGREDIENTS
Serves 4

1 eggplant (aubergine)
salt
2 onions
2 cloves garlic
2 green or red bell peppers (capsicum) —
  or a combination
2 zucchini (courgettes)
3 large ripe tomatoes
⅓ cup (3 fl oz/90 ml) olive oil
freshly ground black pepper
4 sprigs fresh parsley, leaves only, to garnish
  (optional)

TO MAKE

1. Cut eggplant crosswise into ¼ in (5 mm)-thick slices then cut each slice into halves or quarters. Place in a colander, sprinkling layers liberally with salt, and stand in sink or over a bowl 30 minutes to degorge. See page 4.

2. Meanwhile, peel onion and slice into rings. Peel and thinly slice garlic. Halve peppers, remove seeds and cut into thick strips. Cut zucchini crosswise into ½ in (1 cm)-thick rounds. Slice tomatoes.

3. Rinse eggplant under cold running water to remove salt. Drain and dry with paper towels.

4. Drizzle 1 tablespoon oil in a large, heavy-based saucepan, arrange vegetable layers in this order: onion, garlic, bell pepper, eggplant, zucchini, tomatoes. Sprinkle with black pepper to taste and drizzle with remaining oil.

5. Cover pan and cook over low to medium heat, without stirring, 20–30 minutes or until vegetables are tender. Chop parsley and sprinkle over vegetables before serving.

HINTS & TIPS
• Serve with grilled or roasted meats and poultry, or as a meatless main course with pasta **(pictured)**, rice or couscous (page 64–66 and 72). Serve cold as part of an antipasti tray or summer salad platter.
• A splash of red or white wine or lemon juice, a handful of marinated black olives and a sprinkling of chopped fresh or dried herbs (e.g. oregano or basil) can be added in Step 4.
• When ripe fresh tomatoes are not available, use a 14 oz (400 g) can whole, peeled tomatoes. Crush tomatoes before adding. Uncover pan during last 5–10 minutes of cooking to evaporate excess moisture.

Green salad with vinaigrette

INGREDIENTS
Serves 4

4–6 cups prepared mixed fresh salad leaves
   (see below)
1 small purple onion
1 tblspn chopped fresh or ½ tspn dried herb e.g.
   basil, thyme, tarragon, chives, mint (optional)

FOR VINAIGRETTE DRESSING
1 clove garlic
1 tspn Dijon mustard
pinch of sugar
freshly ground black pepper
1 tblspn white or red wine vinegar or lemon juice
¼–⅓ cup (2–3 fl oz/60–90 ml) virgin
   olive oil

TO MAKE
1. For the dressing, peel and halve garlic. Place all ingredients in a screw-top jar. Cover and shake until blended. Or, whisk together first 5 ingredients in a small bowl. Gradually add oil, whisking constantly, until dressing thickens slightly. Stand dressing at room temperature to develop flavors, while preparing salad ingredients. Remove garlic and shake or whisk again before serving.

2. Tear salad leaves into bite-size pieces and place in a salad bowl. Peel onion, slice thinly and separate into rings. Scatter onion and herbs, if using, over salad and mix lightly to combine.

3. Pour dressing over salad, toss lightly and serve immediately.

HINTS & TIPS
• Choose an interesting mix of salad lettuces and leaves for color, flavor and texture. Look for mixed salad leaves at the store — some include edible flower petals, e.g. nasturtiums, marigolds, violets.
• **To prepare leaves:** remove cores by twisting from heads. Separate leaves. Discard any coarse stems or damaged sprigs and rinse under cold running water. Drain well and lightly pat dry with paper towels, a cloth, or use a spin salad basket to remove excess moisture. Wrap loosely in paper towels, seal in plastic bags and refrigerate until crisp.
• Try adding some of the following for extra interest and bulk:
  — blanched and refreshed snow peas (mange tout), asparagus or green beans; sliced celery, radishes, fennel bulb and leaves, mushrooms, scallions (spring onions/shallots), red or green bell pepper (capsicum) strips, shredded carrot.
  — marinated artichoke hearts, black or stuffed green olives, sun-dried tomatoes or peppers (capsicum) in oil, canned anchovy fillets, crumbled feta, goats cheese or sliced bocconcini (fresh mozzarella).
  — sliced grilled beef, leg ham, cooked chicken or turkey, poached fish or canned tuna, hard-cooked (boiled) eggs (hen or quail), canned chickpeas (garbanzo beans), red kidney or cannellini beans;
  — toasted nuts, croûtons
• For a robust garlic flavor, finely chop garlic and let it infuse in oil 1–2 hours before preparing dressing.
• Generally, the ratio of vinegar to oil is one part vinegar to three parts oil, however, you may prefer more or less oil.
• Experiment with a variety of oils and vinegars, including those already flavored with herbs.

Potato salad

Preparation 8 minutes
Cooking time 10–12 minutes
Refrigeration time 1–2 hours

INGREDIENTS
Serves 6–8

2 lb (1 kg) small new potatoes
vinaigrette dressing (page 54)
2 sticks celery
4 scallions (spring onions/shallots) with some
*   green tops*
1 cup purchased or home-made mayonnaise
*   (page 109)*
¹/₂ cup (4 oz/125 ml) sour cream
1¹/₂ tspn Dijon mustard or horseradish cream
freshly ground black pepper
chopped fresh parsley, to serve

TO MAKE

1. Place potatoes in a saucepan of lightly salted water to cover, bring to boil, and cook 10–12 minutes, or until just tender. Drain and cool until easy to handle. Peel, if desired, and cut into thick pieces.

2. Place warm potatoes in a bowl, drizzle with vinaigrette and toss lightly to coat. Cover and refrigerate 1–2 hours or until cold.

3. Trim and slice celery and scallions and add to potatoes.

4. Combine mayonnaise, sour cream and mustard in a bowl. Season to taste with black pepper. Lightly fold mixture through potatoes. Refrigerate until required. Serve well-chilled, sprinkled with parsley.

HINTS & TIPS

• Choose a waxy, red-skinned potato that keeps its shape when cooked. Avoid overcooking — potatoes should be just tender when pierced with a skewer.
• Omit garlic from vinaigrette dressing for milder flavor. Add fresh dill or chives instead.
• Add 6–8 sliced stuffed green olives or 1–2 chopped or sliced hard-cooked (boiled) eggs in Step 3, if desired.
• Change the flavor and color with curry powder or paprika to taste in Step 4.
• Make salad ahead and refrigerate, covered, overnight to let flavors mingle.

Rice or pasta salad

Preparation 8–10 minutes
Cooking time 10–12 minutes
Refrigeration time 1–2 hours

INGREDIENTS
Serves 4–6

8 oz (250 g) long-grain white or brown rice,
*   or small pasta shapes such as penne, spirals,*
*   elbows, shells*
vinaigrette dressing (page 54 — double quantity)
1 purple onion
2–3 sticks celery
4–6 radishes
8–10 black olives, pitted (stoned)
8–10 cherry tomatoes
4 tblspn chopped fresh parsley
lettuce leaves, to serve

TO MAKE

1. Cook rice or pasta in a large saucepan of lightly salted boiling water until tender but still slightly firm to the bite (page 64–66). Drain well. If using pasta, rinse under cold running water and drain again. Transfer to a salad bowl.

2. Prepare a double quantity vinaigrette dressing. Combine with rice or pasta.

3. Peel and thinly slice or finely chop onion. Trim and slice celery and radishes. Halve or thickly slice olives and tomatoes. Add vegetables and chopped parsley to bowl. Toss lightly, cover and refrigerate 1–2 hours.

4. To serve, arrange lettuce in a shallow serving plate or bowl and spoon salad over.

HINTS & TIPS
• Flavors improve if dressing is mixed with warm rice or pasta.
• For a main course salad, add any of the following in Step 4: diced or slivered cooked ham or chicken, drained can of tuna in brine, sliced hard-cooked (boiled) eggs, or toasted pine nuts, walnuts or pecans.
• A little fruit is delicious in a rice salad: golden raisins, chopped dried apricots, canned pineapple pieces or mandarin oranges, fresh orange segments, or diced unpeeled apple.

Marinated bean salad

Preparation 5–10 minutes
Cooking time 5–6 minutes
Refrigeration time 6–12 hours

INGREDIENTS
Serves 6–8
6 oz (180 g) fresh green beans
6 oz (180 g) fresh yellow wax beans
14 oz (400 g) can red kidney beans
14 oz (400 g) can chickpeas (garbanzo beans)
10 oz (300 g) can cannellini or lima beans
1 small green bell pepper (capsicum)
1 purple onion
2 tblspn chopped fresh parsley

FOR SWEET AND TANGY DRESSING
⅓ cup (3 oz/90 g) sugar
⅓ cup (3 fl oz/90 ml) vegetable oil
⅔ cup (5½ fl oz/150 ml) cider vinegar
½ tspn salt
¼ tspn freshly ground black pepper

TO MAKE
1. Trim stem ends from fresh beans. Cut beans diagonally into 2 in (5 cm) lengths. Place in a steamer basket over simmering water in a saucepan, cover and steam 5–6 minutes or until beans are just tender. Drain and refresh under cold running water. Place in a non-metallic bowl.

2. Drain canned beans and peas in a colander and rinse. Drain well and add to fresh beans.

3. Halve bell pepper, remove seeds and cut into ¼ in (5 mm) pieces. Peel and finely chop onion. Add with parsley to bean mixture.

4. To make dressing, place all ingredients in a bowl and stir until blended. Pour over beans and mix well. Cover and refrigerate, stirring once or twice, 6–8 hours or overnight.

5. To serve, stir beans in dressing to coat. Drain well, reserving dressing (see Hints & Tips), and serve.

HINTS & TIPS
• The tangy-sweet dressing makes this a tasty side dish for glazed barbecued chicken, sausages and pork spareribs.
• Use a non-metallic — glass, ceramic or plastic — bowl or container for marinating and storing, as a metal container may react with the vinegar to create a metallic taste.
• If you prefer to use dried beans instead of canned, follow the directions for soaking and cooking on page 67.
• If yellow wax beans aren't available, double the quantity of green beans.
• Return leftover salad to reserved dressing, cover and refrigerate for up to 1 week.

Warm main-course salad

INGREDIENTS
Serves 4
12 oz (375 g) young English spinach
2 oz (60 g) goats or feta cheese

FOR WARM DRESSING
1/3 cup (3 fl oz/90 ml) vegetable or olive oil
1/2 cup (2 oz/60 g) coarsely chopped walnuts
4 slices prosciutto or bacon
1 clove garlic
2–3 tblspn red wine vinegar or lemon juice
1 tspn sugar
1/4 tspn chopped hot red chili or dried chili flakes

TO MAKE

1. Rinse spinach under cold running water, drain and dry with paper towels. Tear larger leaves into bite-size pieces and place in a serving bowl.

2. To make dressing, heat oil in a frying pan over medium heat. Add walnuts and cook, stirring, 1 minute or until golden. Remove pan from heat. Remove nuts immediately with a slotted spoon and scatter over spinach.

3. Cut prosciutto into thick strips. Peel and chop garlic. Return pan to heat and cook prosciutto and garlic, stirring, 2–3 minutes or until prosciutto is crisp and golden.

4. Add vinegar, sugar and chili to pan and simmer, stirring, 30 seconds. Spoon dressing over salad, toss lightly and sprinkle with crumbled cheese. Serve immediately.

HINTS & TIPS
• A "warm" salad is made from just-cooked or room temperature meat, fish or poultry served on a bed of salad leaves and drizzled with a heated dressing.
• Serve as a first course or, with bread, as a light main meal.
• To cook chicken, beef or fish, refer to recipes for Simple Chicken Sauté (page 20), Perfectly Cooked Steaks (page 32), and Grilled, Broiled or Pan-Fried fish (page 12) and reserve cooking juices. Spoon off and discard all fat from juices, and drizzle juices over salad.
• Use an assortment of lettuce leaves mixed with watercress and parsley instead of spinach, if desired.
Add a few blanched and refreshed vegetables such as snow peas (mange tout), green beans or asparagus.

Pasta

Pasta is packaged in various shapes as macaroni or in long, round or flat strands of varying thicknesses as spaghetti or ribbon noodles.

Fresh pasta is usually sold from Italian delicatessens and speciality pasta shops as noodles (fettuccine) or lasagne sheets, or stuffed (with a variety of meat or cheese fillings) and shaped in many guises. Some is made with spinach or tomato paste (concentrate) — among other vegetable additives — to provide attractive colors.

TO COOK PASTA

Use a very large saucepan and 12–16 cups (96–128 fl oz/3–4 litres) water for each 1 lb (500 g) pasta. Bring water to boil with 1 tablespoon oil and salt to taste — oil helps prevent sticking and salt adds flavor. Add pasta, stir, and return to boil. Cook, stirring occasionally, 3–5 minutes for fresh pasta; 10–12 minutes for dried (i.e. packet) pasta or until tender but firm to the bite (al dente). Drain. If serving hot, toss with chosen sauce and serve immediately. If serving cold, rinse under cold running water and drain thoroughly.

NOODLES

Oriental egg noodles can be purchased fresh or dried and are made from wheat flour — just like Italian-style pasta — only the technique for shaping them differs. Dried cellophane (rice stick) noodles can be purchased from oriental food stores and supermarkets. Many brands of quick-cooking noodles are packaged with a flavor sachet and detailed cooking instructions.

TO COOK ORIENTAL NOODLES

• **Fresh or dried egg noodles:** soak in a large bowl of hot water 10 minutes or until they can be separated. Drain.

Cook in plenty of boiling salted water with 1 tablespoon oil 2–4 minutes, depending on thickness, or until just tender but firm to the bite (al dente). Drain, rinse and use as recipes direct — in soups, stir-fries or fried in shallow or deep oil.
• **Cellophane (rice stick) noodles:** add small amounts to shallow hot oil in a wok or large frying pan. They will puff up and crisp quickly. Use as garnishes.

Rice

White (polished) rice is available in short, medium and long grains. Brown rice has been hulled but the bran coating still covers the grain. Wild rice is not a true rice but the seed of a water grass. Both brown and wild rice are prized for their chewy texture and nutty flavor, however they require longer cooking times — up to 45 minutes.
• Short-grain rice clings together and has a creamy texture when cooked. Use it for sweet puddings and oriental dishes to be eaten with chopsticks.
• Medium-grain rice is best for molded rice dishes and savory dumplings or croquettes because when cooked, the grains hold together well. If unavailable, substitute with either short or long-grain rice.
• Long-grain rice cooks into separate, fluffy grains for savory side dishes, poultry stuffings and rice salads.
• Basmati rice, from Pakistan, and jasmine rice, originally from Asia, are varieties of long-grain rice with an aroma that contributes to the flavor of the spiced and fragrant dishes of India and Thailand.
• Arborio rice is a short to medium, plump grain that is most preferred for risottos, as it absorbs liquid without turning mushy. If unavailable, use short-grain rice.

TO COOK RICE

• To remove excess starch and prevent sticking, rinse rice under cold running water until water runs clear. If using brown or wild rice, discard any husks.

• **Rapid boil method:** boil 8 cups (64 fl oz/2 litres) water in a large, heavy-based saucepan. Stir in 1 cup (7 oz/220 g) rice, slowly so that water does not stop boiling. Add salt to taste and boil rapidly, stirring frequently, 10–12 minutes for white rice; 30–45 minutes for brown or wild rice, or until tender but still firm to the bite (al dente). Drain.

• **Absorption method:** boil 2 cups (16 fl oz/ 500 ml) water or stock in a heavy-based saucepan. Stir in 1 cup (7 oz/220 g) rice, slowly so that liquid does not stop boiling. Add salt to taste, cover and reduce heat to very low. Simmer gently 20–25 minutes for white rice; 40–45 minutes for wild rice; 50–55 minutes for brown rice, or until tender and liquid is absorbed. Uncover and fluff rice lightly with a fork. Let stand 5 minutes before serving. If cooking larger quantities, increase water by 1 cup (8 fl oz/250 ml) for each extra cup of rice.

TO MICROWAVE PASTA AND RICE

You won't save much time cooking pasta and rice in the microwave because no matter what cooking method is used, these staples need about the same time to absorb moisture and rehydrate. However, by microwaving rice and packaged pasta, you will avoid messy boil-overs and dirty saucepans. Cooked pasta and rice reheat well in the micro-wave, without glugginess or sticking.

• **For rice:** cover each 1 cup (7 oz/220 g) white rice with 1½ cups (12 fl oz/375 ml) boiling water in a large, deep microwavable bowl. Cover loosely with lid or plastic food wrap. Cook on HIGH (100%) 5–6 minutes, stir, then cook 5–6 minutes more. Let stand, covered, 5 minutes and serve. For brown rice, use 3 cups (24 fl oz/750 ml) water and cook 30 minutes. Let stand 10 minutes.

• **For pasta:** use pasta shapes or break long strands into short lengths, if desired. Cover with enough boiling water to immerse pasta completely. Add 1 tablespoon oil. Cook on HIGH (100%), stirring occasionally, until pasta is just tender. Let stand, covered, 5 minutes to complete cooking. Drain and serve.

TO REHEAT RICE OR PASTA

• Rinse cooked rice or pasta in hot water. Add a little oil to pasta and gently toss. Otherwise, reheat rice or pasta in leftover sauce or gravy.

• **Microwave method:** place in a microwavable bowl or dish. Cover and cook on HIGH (100%) 30–90 seconds, or until heated through.

• **Conventional method:** place in a colander or large sieve over a saucepan containing 1 in (2.5 cm) simmering water. Cover with foil and steam 4–5 minutes, or until heated through.

Beans

Dried beans, peas and lentils are known as legumes or pulses.
• Cooking time will depend on the variety and age. The fresher the product, the shorter the cooking time (best if used within a month).
• Rinse in cold running water. Pick over and discard any which are dark or mishapen.

TO SOAK

• Split peas and lentils don't require soaking, but will cook more quickly and yield a better volume if soaked 1–2 hours in 4 cups (32 fl oz/1 l) water for each 1 cup (6½ oz/200 g) lentils.
• All beans must be soaked before cooking to soften and tenderize them.
Overnight method: place in a large bowl, cover with cold water. Cover bowl and let stand at room temperature overnight (6–8 hours).
• **Quick method:** place in a large saucepan, cover with water and bring to boil. Reduce heat and simmer gently 5 minutes. Remove pan from heat, cover and let stand 1–2 hours.

TO COOK

• Use soaking water or fresh water for cooking as recipes direct.
• Barely cover beans with water in large saucepan. Cover pan, bring to boil and boil 10 minutes. Reduce heat and simmer until tender but not mushy, about 1–1½ hours.
• To avoid toughness, wait until beans are just tender before adding salt, sugar or acids such as tomatoes, lemon juice or vinegar.
• To cook lentils for a salad: add 1 cup (6½ oz/200 g) rinsed lentils (any color) to a saucepan of boiling, lightly salted water. Reduce heat and simmer 15–30 minutes, depending on variety, until just tender — not mushy. Drain.

• Most dried beans, peas and lentils are available presoaked and precooked in cans and can be used instead of home-cooked ones, although the texture is softer and flavor salty. Rinse before using, unless otherwise directed by recipes.

SERVING GUIDE

• **Rice:** use ¼–⅓ cup (2–2½ oz/60–75 g) rice per serving.
• **Pasta:** use 3 oz (90 g) dried pasta or 5 oz (150 g) fresh pasta per serving for a main dish. Decrease this amount by 1–2 oz (30–60 g) if serving as a first course.
• **Beans and peas:** use ¼ cup (2 oz/60 g) dried beans, split peas or lentils to yield ½–⅔ cup (4–5 oz/125–150 g) cooked beans per serving.

Chinese fried rice

INGREDIENTS
Serves 4
2 eggs
pinch of salt
*4 scallions (spring onions/shallots) with
    some green tops*
½ red or green bell pepper (capsicum)
½ stick celery
*4 oz (125 g) roasted or barbecued pork, chicken,
    or leg ham*
3 tblspn peanut or vegetable oil
7 oz (220 g) can shrimp (prawns), drained
3 cups cooked white or brown rice
½ cup (2 oz/60 g) cooked green peas

FOR STIR-FRY SAUCE
2 tblspn chicken stock
1½ tblspn Chinese rice wine or dry sherry
2 tspn soy sauce

TO MAKE
1. Whisk together eggs and salt until blended. Cut scallions, bell pepper, celery and meat into thin slivers.

2. Heat 1 tablespoon oil in a wok or large, heavy-based frying pan over medium heat. Add eggs and cook stirring, until scrambled but not dry. Remove from pan and set aside.

3. Heat remaining oil in pan until hot. Add scallions, vegetables, meat and shrimp and stir-fry 45–60 seconds.

4. Add rice to pan and stir-fry 2–3 minutes, or until rice is heated through. Stir in reserved egg and peas.

5. Stir together sauce ingredients and drizzle over rice. Toss lightly to mix well. Serve immediately.

HINTS & TIPS
• Leftover rice is ideal for this dish. If using freshly cooked rice, it is best to spread it on a tray lined with greaseproof (waxed) paper, cover with a clean cloth and refrigerate several hours to dry out before using.
• You can use up any other leftovers in this dish — roast pork, ham or chicken and cooked vegetables.
• If using frozen peas, there is no need to cook them first, just rinse under hot water and drain before using.
• Soak 4–6 Chinese dried mushrooms in boiling water 30 minutes, drain and discard stalks. Thinly slice mushrooms and stir-fry in Step 3.

Leek and mushroom risotto

INGREDIENTS
Serves 4
1 leek, white part only
1 clove garlic
4-6 oz (125-180 g) button mushrooms
6 cups (48 fl oz/1.5 l) chicken stock
2 oz (60 g) butter
2 cups (14 oz/400 g) arborio or short-grain rice
(page 64)
½ cup (2 oz/60 g) grated parmesan
freshly ground black pepper
parmesan shavings, to serve
chopped fresh parsley, to serve

TO MAKE
1. Halve leek lengthwise and rinse under cold running water. Drain and slice thinly. Peel and slice garlic. Halve or quarter mushrooms, if large.

2. Bring stock to boil in a saucepan over high heat.

3. Meanwhile, melt butter in a large, heavy-based saucepan over medium heat. Add leek, garlic and mushrooms, and cook stirring, 3–5 minutes, or until leek is soft and liquid from mushrooms has evaporated.

4. Add rice and stir until well coated with butter mixture. Reduce heat and stir in 1 cup (8 fl oz/250 ml) boiling stock. Cook gently, stirring occasionally, until stock is absorbed.

5. Continue adding stock and cooking in this way 25–30 minutes or until all stock is absorbed and rice is tender but still firm to the bite (al dente).

6. Stir in grated parmesan and season to taste with pepper. Serve with parmesan shavings and parsley.

HINTS & TIPS
• Add ¼ cup (2 fl oz/60 ml) dry white wine with leeks in Step 3 and evaporate before adding rice.
• When cooked, risotto should have a creamy consistency; if too stiff, stir in a little extra stock in Step 5.
• To make parmesan shavings, use a swivel-bladed vegetable peeler to cut thin shavings from a large piece of fresh, room-temperature cheese.
• Serve with a fresh green salad and crusty bread.

Spiced couscous

Preparation 10–15 minutes
Cooking time 30–35 minutes

INGREDIENTS
Serves 4
1 clove garlic
1 onion
1 small red or green bell pepper (capsicum)
2 cups (16 fl oz/500 ml) chicken stock
2 tblspn olive oil
1/2 tspn ground cumin
1/4 tspn ground cinnamon or garam masala
1/2 tspn grated orange rind
freshly ground black pepper
4 dried apricots
1/4 cup (1 1/2 oz/45 g) golden raisins (sultanas)
1 cup (6 oz/180 g) couscous
2 tblspn chopped fresh mint or cilantro (coriander)
2 boneless skinned chicken breast fillets
finely julienned orange rind, to garnish (optional)

TO MAKE
1. Peel and chop garlic and onion. Halve bell pepper, remove seeds and julienne thinly.

2. Heat stock in small saucepan over medium-high heat.

3. Meanwhile, heat 1 tablespoon oil in a saucepan over medium heat. Add garlic, onion and pepper and cook stirring, 3–5 minutes or until onion is soft.

4. Add hot stock, spices, rind and black pepper to taste to pan. Bring mixture to boil then remove pan from heat.

5. Chop apricots. Add fruit, couscous and mint to pan and mix well. Cover pan and let stand 15 minutes, or until couscous swells and absorbs all liquid.

6. Heat remaining oil in a heavy-based frying pan over medium heat. Add chicken and cook 5–6 minutes on each side, or until cooked through and golden. Remove from pan and let cool slightly.

7. Cut chicken into thin strips, add to couscous mixture and toss lightly. Serve garnished with orange rind.

HINTS & TIPS
• Couscous is fine semolina and looks like a grain. It is often served in place of rice or noodles with saucy meat dishes or vegetable stews e.g. as One-pot Meals (page 36) and Ratatouille (page 52) and takes only minutes to prepare.
• **To prepare couscous for four people:** place 1 1/4 cups (7 1/2 oz/235 g) couscous in a bowl. Stir in 1 1/4 cups (10 fl oz/ 315 ml) boiling stock or water, cover and stand 10 minutes, or until couscous swells and all liquid is absorbed. Fluff lightly with a fork to separate grains. Serve hot or store, covered, in the refrigerator until needed.
• Serve couscous cold mixed with salad ingredients and a dressing; hot as a breakfast porridge with warm milk, butter and brown sugar; or as a pilau mixed with dried fruits, toasted nuts and sautéed onion.

Tomato pasta sauce

Preparation 10–15 minutes
Cooking time 10–12 minutes

INGREDIENTS
Serves 4. Makes 2 cups (16 fl oz/500 ml)
2½ lb (1.25 kg) ripe tomatoes
1 clove garlic
2 tblspn olive oil
2–3 tblspn chopped fresh basil leaves or
    2 tspn dried
1 lb (500 g) pasta, cooked (page 64–66), to serve
chopped fresh basil, to serve
parmesan shavings, to serve

TO MAKE
1. Rinse tomatoes and place 2 or 3 at a time in a saucepan of simmering water 30–45 seconds or until skins begin to break. Remove with a slotted spoon and drain.

2. Use a sharp knife to peel off skins and remove cores; discard. Place tomatoes, in batches, in a blender or food processor and process briefly to make coarse chunks.

3. Peel and slice garlic. Heat oil in a large, heavy-based saucepan over medium heat. Add garlic and sauté 1 minute. Add tomatoes and basil and bring to boil, stirring constantly. Reduce heat and simmer 8–10 minutes or until sauce thickens. Serve with hot cooked pasta, sprinkled with basil and parmesan if desired **(pictured)**.

HINTS & TIPS
• When fully-ripe tomatoes are unavailable, use 2 x 14 oz (400 g) cans whole, peeled, undrained tomatoes. Crush tomatoes or place in a food processor and briefly blend.
• For variety, add 2–3 slices chopped bacon or prosciutto, 6–8 sliced stuffed green olives or 1 teaspoon chopped hot red chili or dried chili flakes to pan when sautéing garlic.

Creamy pasta sauce

Preparation 5 minutes
Cooking time 5–8 minutes

INGREDIENTS
Serves 4. Makes 1¼ cups (10 fl oz/300 ml)
2–3 scallions (spring onions/shallots) with some
    green tops
2 tblspn butter
1½ cups (12 fl oz/375 ml) whipping cream
½–¾ cup (2–3 oz/60-90 g) grated parmesan
pinch ground nutmeg
1 lb (500 g) pasta, cooked (page 64–66), to serve
parmesan shavings, to serve

TO MAKE
1. Cut scallions diagonally into thin slivers. Melt butter in a large heavy-based frying pan over medium heat. Add scallions and cook, stirring, 2–3 minutes or until soft.

2. Add cream, grated cheese and nutmeg to pan and bring slowly to a simmer. Simmer very gently over low heat, stirring constantly, 3–5 minutes or until cheese melts and sauce thickens slightly.

3. Serve immediately with hot cooked pasta, sprinkled with parmesan shavings if desired.

HINTS & TIPS
• To avoid stringiness, keep heat low after cheese is added.
• Try a combination of gorgonzola and parmesan cheeses.
• For variety, add 4 oz (125 g) sliced button mushrooms, handful of frozen or cooked green peas, or some diced leg ham to pan with scallions.

Creamy macaroni and cheese

INGREDIENTS
Serves 6
7 oz (220 g) elbow macaroni
white sauce (page 109 — double quantity)
4 oz (125 g) cream cheese, at room temperature
2 tspn Dijon or wholegrain mustard
8 oz (250 g) grated cheddar
2 tomatoes
2 slices white sandwich bread, crust removed
2 tblspn chopped fresh parsley
2 tblspn melted butter

TO MAKE
1. Preheat oven to 375°F (190°C/Gas 5). Cook macaroni in a large saucepan of boiling, lightly salted water 8–10 minutes or until tender but still firm to the bite (al dente). Drain and return to pan.

2. Meanwhile, prepare a double quantity white sauce. Stir pieces of cream cheese and mustard into sauce after milk. Cook over medium heat, stirring, until sauce is smooth and thick. Remove pan from heat. Add cheddar and stir until melted.

3. Pour sauce over macaroni and mix well. Spread mixture evenly in an 8 cup (64 fl oz/2 l) shallow ovenproof dish. Cut each tomato into 3 or 4 slices and arrange over macaroni.

4. Finely crumble bread with fingers. Combine with parsley and butter and sprinkle over tomatoes.

5. Bake 20–25 minutes, or until mixture is bubbling and top is golden.

HINTS & TIPS
• Any small pasta shapes such as spirals, bow ties or shells can be used in place of elbow macaroni.
• **To microwave the assembled dish:** cook on HIGH (100%) 8–10 minutes, or until heated through and bubbling. If your microwave does not have a turn-table, rotate dish 2 or 3 times during cooking for even heat distribution.

Oriental noodles with vegetables

INGREDIENTS
Serves 4

10 oz (300 g) fine Chinese egg noodles
2 tblspn peanut oil
4 oz (125 g) snow peas (mange tout)
1 red bell pepper (capsicum)
4 oz (125 g) oyster or button mushrooms
4 scallions (spring onions/shallots) with
*   some green tops*
1 clove garlic
1 tblspn peeled, grated fresh ginger
1 tblspn sesame seeds

FOR ORIENTAL DRESSING

1 tblspn chopped fresh cilantro (coriander)
2 tblspn peanut oil
2 tblspn lime or lemon juice
1 tblspn sweet chili sauce
1 tblspn soy sauce, preferably light

TO MAKE

1. Place dressing ingredients in a screw-top jar, cover and shake well to blend.

2. Soak noodles in a bowl of hot water 10 minutes or until strands separate; drain. Cook in a large saucepan of boiling water 2–3 minutes or until tender but still firm to the bite (al dente). Drain and rinse under cold running water. Drain again and toss with 1 tablespoon oil.

3. Meanwhile, trim stem ends from snow peas. Halve pepper, remove seeds and cut into thin strips. Thinly slice mushrooms and scallions. Peel and slice garlic.

4. Heat remaining oil in a wok or large, heavy-based frying pan over high heat. Add ginger and garlic and stir-fry 1 minute.

5. Add snow peas and pepper and stir-fry 2–3 minutes or until snow peas turn bright green.

6. Add mushrooms, scallions, noodles and dressing and heat through, stirring.

7. Spread sesame seeds on baking sheet and toast under hot broiler (grill). Sprinkle onto noodles and serve immediately.

HINTS & TIPS
• Chinese egg noodles can be purchased in bundles in both fine and thicker widths from oriental food stores and supermarkets. If using wide noodles, cook them 3–5 minutes in Step 2.
• Try adding 8–12 oz (250–375 g) flaked poached fish (page 10) or finely sliced cooked chicken (page 20) in Step 6.

Lentils with bacon

INGREDIENTS
Serves 4–6

3 slices bacon
1 large onion
2 cloves garlic
1 small red bell pepper (capsicum)
1 tblspn olive oil
1¼ cups (8 oz/250 g) brown or green lentils,
*   rinsed (page 67)*
1 small bay leaf
2 tspn chopped fresh sage or thyme
*   or ½ tspn dried*
freshly ground black pepper
1½–2 cups (12–16 fl oz/375–500 ml) stock
*   or water*
2 scallions (spring onions/shallots) with
*   some green tops*
2 sprigs fresh parsley or cilantro (coriander),
*   leaves only*

TO MAKE

1. Remove rind from bacon and coarsley chop. Peel and chop onion and garlic. Halve bell pepper, remove seeds and cut into ¼ in (6 mm) pieces.

2. Heat oil in a large, heavy-based saucepan over medium heat. Add bacon and cook, stirring, 1 minute. Add onion, garlic and bell pepper and cook 5 minutes or until onion is golden.

3. Add lentils, bay leaf, herb and black pepper to taste. Add enough stock to barely cover mixture and bring to boil. Reduce heat, cover and simmer gently 30–40 minutes or until lentils are tender — not mushy — and liquid has been absorbed.

4. Thinly slice scallions and chop parsley or cilantro. Sprinkle greens over lentils and serve.

HINTS & TIPS

• Serve with grilled sausages (**pictured**), chicken or burgers.
• Red or yellow lentils can be used instead of brown or green lentils. They are smaller, however, and so cook more quickly and mush if overcooked. Check after 15–20 minutes.
• **To make a salad for four people:** cook lentils following recipe. While still warm, combine with chopped or sliced salad vegetables — purple onion or scallions (spring onions/shallots), parsley or mint, celery, red bell pepper, unpeeled cucumber — and drizzle with vinaigrette dressing (page 54) to which garlic and orange rind have been added. Let stand at room temperature 1 hour before serving to allow flavors to develop.

Split pea and ham soup

INGREDIENTS
Serves 6–8
16 oz (500 g) green or yellow split peas
   (yellow split peas pictured)
8 cups (64 fl oz/2 l) cold water
1 meaty ham bone
2 whole cloves
1 large onion
2 carrots
freshly ground black pepper
croutons to serve (optional)

TO MAKE
1. Rinse peas under cold running water, discarding any dark peas. Place in a large, heavy-based saucepan with water, ham bone and cloves. Peel and finely chop onion and carrots and add to pan.

2. Bring slowly to a boil. Reduce heat, cover and simmer gently 1 hour or until meat begins to fall from bone. Remove bone with tongs. When cool enough to handle, cut meat from bone and chop. Discard bone.

3. Blend soup in blender or food processor. Return to pan and add chopped meat. Cover and simmer, stirring occasionally, 1 hour more or until peas are mushy and soup is the consistency desired. Season to taste with black pepper.

HINTS & TIPS
• You can reduce the simmering time by half by soaking peas in cold water overnight. Drain peas and proceed as directed.
• Use 1–1¼ lb (500–625 g) meaty smoked bacon bones or a smoked pork hock in place of the ham bone.
• Serve with croûtons — slices of buttered toast that have been cut into cubes or fancy shapes such as stars **(pictured)**.

Foolproof pan pizza

INGREDIENTS
Serves 4
2 tblspn olive oil
1²⁄₃ cups (6¹⁄₂ oz/200 g) all-purpose (plain) flour
2 tspn baking powder
1¹⁄₂ tspn sugar
¹⁄₂ tspn salt
²⁄₃ cup (5 fl oz/160 ml) milk

FOR PIZZA TOPPING
1 cups (8 fl oz/250 ml) store-bought tomato
*   pasta sauce*
¹⁄₄ cup (2 oz/60 g) tomato paste (concentrate)
1¹⁄₂ cups (6 oz/180 g) grated mozzarella
2 cups thinly sliced assorted pizza toppings
*   (see below)*

TO MAKE
1. Preheat oven to 425°F (220°C/Gas 7). Place oil in a 10 in (25 cm) round ovenproof shallow pan, tilt to coat base and sides with oil and place in oven to heat 4–5 minutes.

2. Meanwhile, combine flour, baking powder, sugar and salt in a bowl. Make a well in center, pour in milk and mix with a fork, until dry ingredients are just moistened.

3. Turn dough onto a lightly floured surface. Knead gently 1 minute or until smooth. Shape into a 10 in (25 cm) circle.

4. Remove pan from oven and quickly press dough into base and halfway up sides. Bake 10 minutes.

5. To make pizza sauce, mix pasta sauce and tomato paste and spread over partially baked crust. Sprinkle with two-thirds of the cheese. Arrange other toppings on pizza and sprinkle with remaining cheese.

6. Bake 20–25 minutes more, or until crust is cooked through and cheese melted. Let cool briefly before cutting.

HINTS & TIPS
• Use any 9–10 in (23–25 cm) diameter ovenproof pan e.g. a cast-iron frying pan, 3–4 in (8–10 cm) deep cake or springform pan or ceramic baking dish.
• **To make your own tomato pasta sauce for topping:** combine 1 cup (8 fl oz/250 ml) tomato ketchup, ³⁄₄ cup (6 fl oz/180 ml) tomato paste, 1 teaspoon each dried basil and oregano leaves, 1 finely chopped clove garlic and black pepper to taste. Or use recipe for tomato pasta sauce on page 74, simmered until quite thick.
• Pizza toppings can include thinly sliced button mushrooms, pepperoni sausage or salami, bell pepper (capsicum), pitted (stoned) black olives, or drained canned pineapple chunks.

Quiche with saucepan pastry

Preparation 10–15 minutes
Cooking time 40–45 minutes

INGREDIENTS
Serves 6

3–4 slices bacon
½ bunch scallions (spring onions/shallots), with
some green tops
1½ cups (6 oz/180 g) grated cheddar or
swiss cheese
3 eggs
¾ cup (6 fl oz/180 ml) milk
¾ cup (6 fl oz/180 ml) whipping cream
1 tblspn all-purpose (plain) flour
2 tspn Dijon mustard
freshly ground black pepper

FOR PASTRY
⅔ cup (5 fl oz/160 ml) milk
4 oz (125 g) butter, cut into pieces
2 cups (8 oz/250 g) all-purpose (plain) flour
1½ tspn baking powder
pinch of salt

HINTS & TIPS
• Avoid overmixing the pastry or it will be tough.
• Instead of scallions, substitute 10 oz (300 g) frozen chopped spinach which has been thawed and squeezed dry; a combination of cooked green peas and whole kernel corn; 1–1¼ cups (10–12 oz/315–375 ml) chopped cooked vegetable e.g. broccoli.
• Instead of bacon, use 6–8 oz (180–250 g) diced leg ham, thinly sliced cooked chicken or drained canned red salmon or chunk-style tuna.

TO MAKE

1. To make pastry, warm milk and butter in a large saucepan over medium heat until butter just melts. Remove from heat and let cool slightly.

2. Sift together flour, baking powder and salt. Add, all at once, to milk mixture. Beat with a wooden spoon until just blended and smooth. Press warm mixture evenly into base and sides of a 10 in (25 cm) fluted pie (flan) ring with removable base. Trim edges to rim of pan with a sharp knife.

3. Preheat oven to 400°F (200°C/Gas 6).

4. To make filling, remove rind from bacon and coarsely chop. Heat a small frying pan over medium heat. Add bacon and sauté until just golden. Remove bacon with a slotted spoon and scatter over pastry. Thinly slice scallons. Scatter with cheese over bacon.

5. Whisk together eggs, milk, cream, flour, mustard and black pepper. Carefully pour mixture over filling.

6. Bake 10 minutes. Reduce oven temperature to 350°F (180°C/Gas 4) and bake 30–35 minutes or until filling is set and pastry crusty and golden. Let stand 5–10 minutes in pan to let filling settle. Cut into wedges to serve.

Pastry parcels

INGREDIENTS
Serves 6
filling (see opposite and Hints & Tips)
12 sheets phyllo pastry
vegetable oil
flaked almonds
sugar

TO MAKE
1. Prepare filling as recipe directs.

2. Preheat oven to 375°F (190°C). Cut pastry sheets crosswise in half then cover with a cloth to prevent drying. Working quickly, layer a stack of four pastry pieces for each parcel, brushing every second sheet lightly with oil.

3. Divide filling into six equal portions. Spoon one portion onto center of each stack. Lift four corners of pastry to meet over filling and gently press together to form a parcel.

4. Brush parcels lightly with oil. Sprinkle with almonds and sugar. Place on a lightly greased baking sheet.

5. Bake 15–20 minutes, or until pastry is golden brown. Serve warm — accompany with ice cream or custard, if desired.

For cherry filling

INGREDIENTS
14 oz (440 g) can pitted sour (morello) cherries
2 oz (60 g) sugar
2 tblspn cornstarch (cornflour)
1 tblspn butter
2–3 drops vanilla or almond extract (essence)

TO MAKE
1. Drain cherries, reserving 1 cup (8 fl oz/ 250 ml) liquid.

2. Combine sugar and cornstarch in a small saucepan. Stir in reserved liquid. Cook over medium heat, stirring constantly, until sauce boils and thickens. Cook, stirring 1 minute more.

3. Remove from heat. Stir in cherries, butter and extract to taste. Cool. Use as directed.

HINTS & TIPS
• Pastry parcels can also contain savory fillings. Try the following as an appetizer for 6 people. Divide 12 uncooked, shelled, medium shrimp (prawns) in half lengthwise. Coat in a mixture of 1 clove chopped garlic, ¾ cup (3 oz/90 g) dried breadcrumbs, 4 tablespoons chopped fresh parsley, 3 tablespoons grated parmesan, pinch cayenne pepper and 2–3 oz (60–90 g) melted butter (enough to moisten mixture). Place 4 shrimp halves on each pastry stack. Sprinkle parcels with sesame seeds instead of almonds and sugar.

Butter cake with cream cheese frosting

INGREDIENTS

1/2 cup (4 oz/125 g) butter, softened
1 tspn vanilla extract (essence)
3/4 cup (6 oz/180 g) superfine (caster) sugar
2 eggs
1 1/2 cups (6 oz/180 g) all-purpose (plain) flour
1 1/2 tspn baking powder
1/2 cup (4 fl oz/125 ml) milk

FOR CREAM CHEESE FROSTING

1/2 cup (4 oz/125 g) cream cheese, at room
   temperature
1 tspn vanilla extract (essence)
1 1/2 cups (8 oz/250 g) confectioners (icing) sugar
2–3 tblspn cream or milk

HINTS & TIPS

• This batter makes enough for one 3–4 in (7.5–10 cm)
deep, 8 in (20 cm) round cake layer pan or kugelhopf
mold; one 5 x 9 in (14 x 21 cm) loaf pan or 12–15 standard
cupcakes. To prevent spillovers, fill pans no more than
two-thirds full.
• To prepare a pan for baking, grease a flat-bottomed
baking pan by rubbing it with butter or margarine and
line the base with greased parchment (baking) paper. Dust
a greased mold lightly with flour, and use paper liners in
cupcake pans. This enables easy removal of the cake.
• To test a cake, insert a wooden skewer or toothpick into
center; it is cooked if the skewer comes out clean. The top
should spring back when gently pressed with a fingertip
and it should begin to pull from sides of pan.
• **For chocolate cake:** add 2 tablespoons sifted cocoa or
2 oz (60 g) melted, cooled dark bittersweet chocolate.
To the frosting, add 1–2 tablespoons sifted cocoa or 1 oz
(30 g) melted, cooled dark bittersweet chocolate.

TO MAKE

1. Preheat oven to 350°F (180°C/Gas 4).
Place butter and vanilla in a bowl and, using an
electric mixer, beat until creamy. Beat in sugar,
2 tablespoons at a time, until light and fluffy.
Add eggs, one at a time, beating well after
each addition.

2. Sift together flour with baking powder and,
using a wooden spoon, stir about one-third
into creamed mixture until just blended.
Add one-third milk and stir until smooth.
Repeat procedure twice, using remaining flour
and milk.

3. Prepare a baking pan (see Hints & Tips).
Spread mixture into pan and bake 60 minutes
for loaf; 40–45 minutes for cake pan or
kugelhopf mold; 18–20 minutes for cupcakes
— or until cake is cooked when tested
(see Hints & Tips).

4. Cool cake in pan 5 minutes. Run a metal
spatula around edge of pan to loosen cake.
Turn onto a wire rack. Peel off lining paper
and let cool completely.

5. To make frosting, place cream cheese and
vanilla in a mixing bowl and, using an electric
mixer, beat until creamy and light. Add
confectioners sugar and cream or milk and
beat until mixture is a good consistency for
spreading. Spread over cooled cake.

Muffins

INGREDIENTS
Makes 9 large or 18 small muffins
1¾ cups (7 oz/220 g) all-purpose (plain) flour
¼ cup (2 oz/60 g) superfine (caster) sugar
1½ tspn baking powder
½ tspn salt
1 egg
¾ cup (6 fl oz/180 ml) milk
90 g (3 oz) butter, melted

TO MAKE
1. Preheat oven to 425°F (220°C/Gas 7). Grease nine 2¾ in (7 cm)-diameter muffin cups or 18 small cupcake cups, or line with paper cups.

2. Sift together flour, sugar, baking powder and salt into a large mixing bowl and make a well in center.

3. Combine egg, milk and melted butter. Pour into well and, using a fork, mix lightly 30 seconds or until dry ingredients are just moistened — mixture should be lumpy.

4. Spoon batter into prepared cups, filling two-thirds full. Bake until browned, 15–20 minutes for large; 12–15 minutes for small. Serve warm.

HINTS & TIPS
• Serve with butter, jam or jelly if desired.
• **For self-rising muffins:** use self-rising (self-raising) flour and omit the baking powder.
• **For cheese muffins:** reduce sugar to 1 tablespoon and stir ½ cup (2 oz/60 g) grated mature cheddar or Swiss cheese into dry ingredients.
• **For herb muffins:** reduce sugar to 1 tablespoon and stir 3–4 tablespoons chopped mixed fresh (or 2 teaspoons dried) herbs e.g. parsley, oregano, chives, sage, dill in Step 3.
• **For fruit muffins:** add ½–¾ cup (4–6 oz/ 125–180 g) chopped seedless raisins, pitted (stoned) dates or dried apricots to dry ingredients.
• **For jam muffins:** fill baking cups with batter and place 1 teaspoon jelly (jam) in center of each before baking.
• **For apple spice muffins:** half-fill baking cups with batter, top each with 2 teaspoons canned apple pie filling, then cover with remaining batter. Sprinkle muffins with a mixture of ground cinnamon and superfine (caster) sugar before baking.

HINTS & TIPS

• Cooking times are based on large-size (2 oz/60 g), room-temperature eggs. If cold, rinse eggs briefly under warm running water.
• To test for freshness, place an egg in a glass of cold water. A fresh egg will sink immediately to the bottom; a bad egg floats. If the egg is older than 1 week, it will stand pointed end down near the bottom of the glass.
• The color of an eggshell reflects the breed of the hen, not nutritional value or freshness.

SCRAMBLED EGGS

• Place 1 tablespoon milk for each egg in a bowl, add desired number of eggs with salt and freshly ground black pepper to taste and whisk to combine. Melt about $\frac{1}{2}$ teaspoon butter for each egg in a heavy-based saucepan over low heat. Add egg mixture and cook, occasionally stirring gently, until mixture is set but still creamy. Serve immediately.
• **Microwaved:** Melt 2 teaspoons butter in a small, microwavable dish. Whisk together 2 eggs, 2–3 tablespoons milk and freshly ground black pepper to taste. Add to dish. Cook on MEDIUM (50%), stirring once or twice, $1\frac{1}{2}$–2 minutes or until set but still creamy.
• **Serving suggestions:** for a gourmet brunch or supper dish, add one of the following combinations to scrambled eggs. Heat through and serve with toasted bagels or another interesting type of bread:
— bacon, parsley and cracked pepper.
— strips of smoked salmon, snipped fresh chives, freshly ground black pepper **(pictured)**.
— grated gruyère or emmenthal cheese, sautéed mushrooms and steamed fresh asparagus spears.
— finely chopped sun-dried tomatoes, red and green bell pepper (capsicum), and scallions (shallots/spring onions) with grated mature cheddar cheese and a dash of hot pepper sauce.

POACHED EGGS

• Half-fill a frying pan with water and bring to a simmer. Add 1 tablespoon white vinegar or lemon juice — a little acid helps the egg hold its shape. Break eggs, one at a time, into a cup and carefully slide out into water. Cook, basting yolks occasionally, 3–4 minutes or until yolks set as desired. Using a slotted spoon, remove eggs, drain briefly and trim off any ragged edges. Serve immediately.
• **Microwave:** quarter-fill a small soufflé cup or ramekin with hot water and heat on HIGH (100%) 30–60 seconds or until boiling. Add egg and, using a skewer or sharp knife, pierce yolk in several places. Cook on MEDIUM-HIGH (70%) 45–60 seconds or until cooked as desired.
• **For Eggs Benedict:** poach 2 eggs and serve them on a split, toasted English muffin which has been topped with cooked lean bacon or ham. Spoon hollandaise sauce (page 108) over eggs and serve immediately **(pictured page 2)**.
• **For Eggs Florentine:** omit ham and top muffins with cooked, well-drained English spinach.

BOILED EGGS

• **Soft:** bring a saucepan of water to boil then reduce heat to simmer. Using a slotted spoon, lower eggs carefully into pan and cook to your liking — 3–4 minutes for soft set; 4–5 minutes for firmer set.
• **Hard:** arrange eggs snugly in a saucepan, pointed end down (this helps keep yolks in middle of whites). Add cold water to cover eggs and bring to boil. Boil 10 minutes. Drain and cool under cold running water. Peel immediately for best results. Note that when overcooked, a green ring of iron sulfide forms around yolk. This is harmless but can be avoided if you observe the cooking time and cool eggs quickly.
• **Microwave:** use only a special microwave egg boiler as manufacturer directs.

French omelette

INGREDIENTS
Serves 1
2 eggs
1 tblspn cold water
pinch of salt
freshly ground black pepper
2 tspn butter

TO MAKE
1. Place eggs, water, salt and pepper to taste in a bowl and whisk lightly to combine.

2. Melt butter in a 7–8 in (18–20 cm) omelette pan or small frying pan over medium-low heat, until butter is foaming. Tilt pan to coat bottom completely with butter.

3. Pour in egg mixture and cook, stirring once or twice, 1 minute. Cook without stirring, 2–3 minutes more or until eggs are cooked as desired — use a metal spatula or knife to lift edges occasionally, allowing uncooked mixture to flow underneath,

4. To serve, tilt pan away from you. Fold the upper third of omelette (closest to the handle) over middle third, tip pan and roll omelette onto a serving plate. Serve immediately.

HINTS & TIPS
• Avoid cooking omelette over too high heat or for too long as it will become tough and dry. Eggs should be just set but still moist on the top and firm and golden on bottom.
• Use 1–2 tablespoons of any of the following, spooned over as omelette cooks, folded in as a filling, or as a topping or side dish: crumbled cooked bacon, sautéed sliced mushrooms, grated cheese, chopped scallions (spring onions/shallots), chopped fresh herbs e.g. basil, parsley, cilantro (coriander), chives, dill or mint, or chopped tomato sautéed with garlic and basil.

Breakfast with the works

Preparation 10 minutes
Cooking time 12–15 minutes

INGREDIENTS
Serves 4
8 fat-trimmed bacon slices or breakfast sausages
4 medium tomatoes
2 tspn vegetable or olive oil
freshly ground black pepper
2 tspn chopped fresh basil or parsley
1 tblspn butter
4 large eggs
8 slices wholemeal (whole wheat) bread
hot pepper sauce, Worcestershire sauce or ketchup
   (tomato sauce) to serve

TO MAKE
1. Preheat oven to 275°F (140°C/Gas 1). Arrange bacon or sausages on a broiler (grill) tray and cook under a preheated medium broiler, turning once or twice, 3–5 minutes or until cooked. Transfer to a serving platter and keep warm in oven.

2. Halve tomatoes and place on tray, brush with oil, sprinkle with pepper and broil (grill) 2–3 minutes or until heated through and bubbly. Add to platter with bacon or sausages, sprinkle with basil or parsley and keep warm in oven.

3. Melt butter in a large, heavy-based frying pan over medium heat until foaming. Break eggs, one at a time, into a cup then carefully slide into pan. Cook eggs until whites are set and yolks still soft for "sunny-side up" (cover pan briefly to help set yolks). For eggs "over easy", flip and cook 20–30 seconds more.

4. Meanwhile, toast bread slices each side.

5. To serve, arrange bacon or sausages, tomatoes and eggs on heated serving plates. Serve immediately with toast and desired sauce.

HINTS & TIPS
• To prevent whites spreading, use special metal egg rings, available from supermarkets and stores selling cooking utensils. Place rings in buttered pan, crack one egg into each and cook as directed above.

Old-fashioned baked apples

INGREDIENTS
Serves 4
4 large cooking apples
4 tblspn chopped seedless raisins
2 tblspn soft brown sugar
2 tblspn brandy or rum
1 oz (30 g) butter, softened
1 cup (8 fl oz/250 ml) hot water or
  apple juice
ground cinnamon and nutmeg
whipped cream, to serve (optional)

TO MAKE
1. Preheat oven to 400°F (200°C/Gas 4). Use an apple corer or a sharp knife to cut around the core of each apple from the top; remove core. Use a vegetable peeler to remove skin from upper third of each apple. Place in a baking dish.

2. Place raisins, sugar, brandy and butter in a bowl, mix well and spoon into cavities of apples. Pour hot water or warmed apple juice into dish and lightly sprinkle apples with spices to taste.

3. Cover with foil and bake 30 minutes. Remove foil and spoon cooking juices over apples. Re-cover and bake 30–35 more minutes or until apples are tender. Serve with cream, if desired.

HINTS & TIPS
• For best results, choose a tart apple variety that holds its shape during cooking, such as Granny Smith, Golden Delicious or Rome Beauty.
• Serve hot or cold, with or without cream.
• Rather than using brandy or rum, these apples are just as wonderful moistened with fresh orange juice or water mixed with a drop or two of vanilla extract (essence).
• **A fast microwave method:** fill apples and place in a deep, microwavable dish. Drizzle apples with water or apple juice, sprinkle with spices, and cover dish with lid or microwavable plastic wrap. Cook on HIGH (100%) 7–8 minutes or until apples are tender.

Lemon sponge pudding

INGREDIENTS
Serves 6
$^2/_3$ cup (6$^1/_2$ oz/200 g) sugar
$^1/_4$ cup (2 oz/60 g) all-purpose (plain) flour
1$^1/_2$ oz (45 g) butter, melted
2 tspn finely grated lemon rind
$^1/_4$ cup (2 fl oz/60 ml) fresh lemon juice
3 eggs
1$^1/_2$ cups (12 fl oz/375 ml) milk
pinch of salt
confectioners (icing) sugar, for dusting

TO MAKE
1. Preheat oven to 375°F (190°C/Gas 5). Combine sugar and flour in a mixing bowl. Add melted butter, lemon rind and juice and mix using a wooden spoon.

2. Separate eggs. Reserve whites. Mix yolks and milk in a small bowl, then stir into flour mixture.

3. Using an electric mixer, beat egg whites with salt until they stand upright in moist, stiff peaks. Add whites to batter and, using a metal spoon or spatula, fold in lightly until no white streaks remain.

4. Pour batter into a lightly greased 4–5 cup (32–40 oz/1–1.25 l) ovenproof dish. Place dish in a large, shallow baking pan and pour 1 in (2.5 cm) hot water into pan.

5. Bake 35–40 minutes or until top is golden and springy to the touch — the pudding will separate into a layer of sauce below a layer of cake. Sift confectioners sugar over pudding and serve warm.

HINTS & TIPS
• Also known as pudding cake, self-saucing pudding, or Lemon Delicious, this dessert can be accompanied by lots of ice cream or sweetened whipped cream.
• **To separate eggs:** gently crack each egg on rim of a small mixing bowl and, holding half the shell in fingers of each hand, slip yolk from shell to shell, letting white fall into bowl. Place yolk in a separate small bowl. Take care not to break yolks or mix with white — the smallest amount will prevent whites beating adequately.

Classic chocolate mousse

INGREDIENTS
Serves 6

10 oz (300 g) semi-sweet (plain) chocolate
4 eggs
3 oz (90 g) butter, at room temperature
1 tblspn brandy or dark rum
1 cup (8 fl oz/250 ml) heavy (double) cream
2 tblspn sugar
chocolate curls (see Hints & Tips), to decorate

HINTS & TIPS

• **To melt chocolate in microwave:** break chocolate into
a microwavable bowl and heat on HIGH (100%), stirring
every 20 seconds, 1¼–1½ minutes. Stir again and if not
melted, heat 20–30 seconds more. Remember chocolate
holds its shape and can easily burn if not stirred
frequently.
• **To make chocolate curls:** use a swivel-bladed vegetable
peeler to shave curls from the sides of a block of room-
temperature chocolate. The colder the chocolate, the more
brittle the curls.
• Substitute very strong black coffee or an orange liqueur
e.g. Grand Marnier or Cointreau for brandy or rum.
• Purchase a 7–8 in (18–20 cm) layer of sponge cake.
Place it in a springform pan (the same size as the cake),
lined on the base with baking (parchment) or waxed paper.
Drizzle cake with a little brandy or rum then spread
mousse evenly over top. Refrigerate. Remove from pan
and decorate as desired with chocolate curls, sifted
confectioners (icing) sugar or whipped cream.

TO MAKE

1. Break or chop chocolate into pieces and
place in a heatproof bowl or the top of a double
boiler. Set bowl over a saucepan filled with
1 in (2.5 cm) barely simmering water — water
should not touch the bowl. Heat, stirring,
until melted and smooth. Remove bowl from
heat and cool chocolate until lukewarm but
still fluid.

2. Separate eggs (page 102), placing whites in
a mixing bowl. Add yolks, one at a time, to
chocolate and beat with a wooden spoon until
blended. Cube butter and add with brandy to
mixture. Beat until smooth.

3. Place cream in a mixing bowl and, using an
electric mixer, beat until it stands in soft curled
peaks. Add to chocolate mixture and, using a
metal spoon or spatula, fold in until no white
streaks remain.

4. Thoroughly wash and dry beaters. Beat egg
whites until they curl in soft, moist peaks when
beaters are lifted. Sprinkle sugar over whites
and continue beating until they stand upright
in stiff peaks. Add to chocolate mixture and
lightly fold in.

5. Spoon mousse into a serving bowl or
individual dessert glasses and refrigerate
until set — at least several hours or overnight.
Decorate with chocolate curls before serving.

Baked cheesecake

Preparation 10 minutes
Cooking time 25–40 minutes
Refrigeration time 6–12 hours

INGREDIENTS
Serves 8
¹/₂ cup (4 oz/125 g) butter
6 oz (180 g) plain sweet cookies (biscuits) e.g.
  chocolate wafers, graham crackers, shortbread
¹/₂ tspn ground cinnamon or nutmeg

FOR CHEESE FILLING
1 lb (500 g) cream cheese, at room temperature
³/₄ cup (6 oz/180 g) sugar
1 tspn finely grated lemon rind
1 tblspn lemon juice
1¹/₂ tspn vanilla extract (essence)
2 eggs

FOR SOUR CREAM TOPPING
1¹/₂ cups (12 oz/375 g) sour cream
2 tblspn sugar
¹/₂ tspn vanilla extract (essence)

HINTS & TIPS
• Use your microwave to quickly melt butter and soften cheese: cut butter or cheese into cubes and place in separate, suitably sized microwavable dishes. Heat on HIGH (100%) 15–20 seconds to melt butter; 20–25 seconds to soften cheese, stirring once after 15 seconds.
• To remove cheesecake from pan, run a flexible metal spatula around edge of pan to loosen cake, then ease springlock open. Holding base of pan in one hand, let ring drop. Use a wide metal spatula to loosen base of cheesecake and carefully lift and slide cake onto serving plate.
• For a special presentation, garnish servings with mint sprigs, strawberries, raspberries, peaches, sliced mangoes or blueberries (pictured).
• Omit the sour cream topping and serve cheesecake sprinkled with ground nutmeg and a dollop of whipped cream on the side.

TO MAKE
1. To make crust, melt butter in a small saucepan over medium heat. Break cookies into a food processor and finely crush using pulse action — or place cookies between two sheets of plastic wrap and crush with a rolling pin.

2. Combine crumbs, cinnamon and butter in a bowl and mix with a fork until crumbs are moistened. Using fingertips, press mixture evenly into base and 2 in (5 cm) up sides of a 9 in (23 cm) springform pan. Refrigerate.

3. Preheat oven to 375°F (190°C/Gas 5).

4. To make filling, combine cream cheese, sugar, lemon rind, juice and vanilla in a bowl. Beat with an electric mixer on medium speed, until just smooth. Add eggs, one at a time, beating slowly after each addition, until just blended. Avoid overbeating (it will cause the filling to crack when baked).

5. Pour filling into crust. Bake 20–30 minutes or until a knife inserted just off-center comes out almost clean. Remove from oven, place on a wire rack and let cool to room temperature.

6. Preheat oven to 425°F (220°C/Gas 7).

7. To make topping, stir together sour cream, sugar and vanilla until smooth. Spread mixture evenly over top of cheesecake and bake 5–8 minutes, or until topping is melted. Let cool again to room temperature.

8. Cover cake with plastic wrap — supported by toothpicks or short wooden skewers if necessary to prevent damage to topping — and refrigerate overnight. Remove cake from pan and cut into thin wedges to serve.

White sauce

Makes 1 cup (8 fl oz/250 ml)

1. Melt 2 tablespoons butter in a saucepan over medium heat. Add 2 tablespoons all-purpose (plain) flour and, using a whisk or wooden spoon, cook, stirring, 1 minute.
2. Remove pan from heat. Gradually blend in 1 cup (8 fl oz/250 ml) warmed milk. Return pan to heat and cook, stirring constantly, until sauce bubbles and thickens. Season to taste with salt and ground white or black pepper.

HINTS & TIPS

• **Optional extras:** 1–2 tablespoons lemon juice, dry sherry or chopped fresh parsley, dill or chives; 1–2 teaspoons Dijon or mild English mustard or Worcestershire sauce; $1/2$–1 teaspoon curry paste; pinch of cayenne pepper.
• **Béchamel sauce:** add 1 bay leaf, 1 slice onion and pinch nutmeg to milk as it heats. Strain before using.
• **Cheese sauce:** prior to serving, stir $1/2$ cup (2 oz/60 g) grated parmesan, mature cheddar or emmenthal into sauce until melted.

Mint sauce

Makes about $1/4$ cup (2 fl oz/60 ml)

1. Wash 8–10 fresh mint leaves, dry with paper towels and chop finely. Place in a bowl, add 1 tablespoon boiling water and 1 teaspoon sugar. Stir until sugar dissolves.
2. Add 1 tablespoon vinegar. Cover and let stand 20 minutes.
3. Serve at room temperature with roast, grilled or broiled lamb.

Mayonnaise

Makes 1 cup (8 fl oz/250 ml)

1. Place 2 egg yolks, 1 tablespoon Dijon mustard, 1 teaspoon lemon juice or white vinegar, $1/2$ teaspoon salt and a pinch of ground white or cayenne pepper in a food processor and blend 5 seconds.
2. With motor running, slowly add 1 cup (8 fl oz/250 ml) olive oil, a little at a time, blending until each amount is absorbed before adding more. Continue blending until all oil is added and sauce is thick.
3. Add 1 teaspoon extra lemon juice or vinegar. If too thick, stir in 1 tablespoon hot water.

HINTS & TIPS

• Refrigerate in a covered, non-metallic container.
• Use a mixture of olive and salad oil if a milder flavor is preferred.
• If you prefer not to make your own mayonnaise, try to use a commercial mayonnaise made with whole eggs.
• **Tartare sauce:** prepare mayonnaise and stir in 2 tablespoons chopped sweet pickle or gherkin relish, 1 tablespoon each chopped fresh parsley, stuffed green olives and capers and a few drops worcestershire sauce.

Index

ACKNOWLEDGMENTS

"Esse Range", Myer Grace Brothers, Sydney NSW Australia
Bed Bath n' Table, Mosman NSW Australia
Blues Point Living, McMahons Point NSW Australia
Country Road Homewares Mosman NSW Australia
Freedom Furniture Pty Ltd, Crows Nest NSW Australia
G & C Ventura P/L, Lilyfield NSW Australia
Kitchen Kapers, Crows Nest NSW Australia
Sirocco Homewares Australia, Willoughby NSW Australia
Ware Unique, Neutral Bay NSW Australia
Wok Wicker & Spice, Glebe NSW Australia

Published by Harbour Books
an imprint of Lansdowne Publishing Pty Ltd
Level 5, 70 George Street, Sydney NSW 2000, Australia

First published 1996

© Copyright: Lansdowne Publishing Pty Ltd

Chief Executive Publisher: Jane Curry
Publishing Manager: Deborah Nixon
Production Manager: Sally Stokes
Project Co-ordinator: Kirsten Tilgals
Designer: Megan Smith
Photographer: John Hollingshead
Stylist and Recipe Editor: Kay Francis

Set in Goudy on Quark Xpress
Printed in Singapore by Tien Wah Press (Pte) Ltd

National Library of Australia Cataloguing-in-Publication data
Venturoni-Wilson, Linda.
The beginner's cookbook.
Includes index.
ISBN 1 86302 499 9
1. Cookery. 2. Kitchen utensils. I. Title.
641.512